THE PRAIRIE TIDES

The Ebbs and Flows of an Era

Don Larsen

Foreword by
Bill Meyer

**ACTIVE
BOOKS**

The Prairie Tides
Don Larsen

First printing November 2005

Library of Congress Control Number: 2005931026

ISBN 0-9746675-5-2

Book Cover Design & Layout by Larry G. Nichols II,
Printed in U.S.A. by Mennonite Press, Inc., Newton, KS 67114

Foreword

T he only thing that doesn't change is change. Things are in a constant state of flow, now more than ever.

When Don Larsen looks over his shoulder to decades ago, growing up in a small rural community in Kansas, and compares then to now following a long distinguished career in elementary education administration, he must be shocked though pleased.

The Prairie Tides tells the story of a small community in flat Kansas. Rippling wheat fields have often been compared to waves on the ocean near where he eventually "settled" in California.

Larsen's family came from the Old Country. Hard work and patience produced a prosperous farm where the family was highly regarded in the community.

Those who remember how it "used to be," or those who never knew, will relish reading this series of stories.

As editor of the local newspaper near where Larsen grew up, after more than five decades it is recalled how mail delivery was twice a day in town and there were two star routes serving the communities of the county. Today we can e-mail a letter to London in nano-seconds or send a package to San Francisco overnight, but find it difficult to get our newspaper delivered by mail to farm homes a few miles away.

Change has brought progress as well as produced frustration. We can send man to the moon but experience problems on the eight lane freeway which becomes a public parking lot twice daily.

The people living in the rural Kansas community where the Larsen family became Americanized will enjoy his book, as will those of later generations everywhere who are genuinely interested in how "things" used to be.

Bill Meyer
Newspaper Publisher
Marion, Kansas

66 *The Prairie Tides* describes the richness of the American midwest during the 1900s. It follows young Andy Larsen as he leaves Denmark to seize the American "opportunity," putting down family roots in rural Kansas, and with pure determination made that opportunity his own. Grandson, Don Larsen, vividly describes details of family farm life, generations of family growth, small town humor and tricks, the usual local characters, and the evolution of small agricultural towns. The final chapters bring into sharp focus the flood tide of immigration and growth, the high tide of midwestern settlement, and the ebb tide as family farms give way to advances in food production and transportation. This is a "for sure" read for anyone with a midwestern heritage. 99

— **Eugene A. Miller**,
publisher and author,
Photographer of the Early West

I wish to dedicate this work
to my Jacquie, who worked with
and believed in me as we worked
Grandpa's sod.

Don

Special Thanks

I wish to thank a number of people making this work possible. They have helped make the story richer and more accurate. Jacquie Larsen, Barbara Gilson, Ann Peters, Barry Schrader, Larry Larsen, Bill Meyer, Marilyn Jones, Donna Larsen, Nancy O'Connell, Margaret Lucke, copy editor, and Judy Entz and her team at The Mennonite Press.

Thanks
Don

Nancy is at my teacher for Positas show

About the Author

Don began learning about life as a barefoot boy on section thirteen, Catlin Township, Marion County, Kansas. Upon completing studies at Kansas State College, he farmed with his father and later taught in a one-room school in the neighboring hamlet of Aulne.

He enjoyed teaching, whether in a 4-H club where he and Jacquie served as leaders or as a Sunday school class teacher. He taught the district 13, one room school in Aulne and city school in Peabody, Kansas, before moving into the school system in Livermore, California.

Art had always been one of Don's favorite activities and soon he was active in the Northern California art scene, serving as an officer, demonstrator, and judge for several groups. He is proud of earning a signature status in two national societies.

Retiring early as a school principal, he founded a family house-inspection business where he still serves in marketing. As he finishes his septuagenarian years he has turned to writing and publishing with Active Books, a company he formed to publish his first book, *I've Never Been an Old Man.*

Books by Don Larsen

I've Never Been an Old Man
The Prairie Tides

Don Larsen, Active Books
358 Lincoln Avenue
Livermore, CA 94550

Phone/Fax (925) 447-5898
        (800) 481-7638
donlarsen@active-books.com
www.active-books.com

Table of Contents

Preface

Tide: Definition: Anything that rises and falls or comes and goes. There's been a lot of tides in the prairie country that stretches from Canada's prairie provinces through the Texas plains, and from eastern Colorado across Indiana.

Change has always been a part of American life. The speed of change varies, but forces present themselves to improve, refine, or lessen problems or pains. Sometimes the change can be severe, perhaps even leading to a decline. The whaling industry grew, prospered, and waned, as did the Mississippi steamboat era. Forty-niner gold mining grew rapidly and stopped, only to revive itself whenever gold prices rose again, but each revival was somewhat different from the previous outbreaks of gold fever.

When John Deere invented the steel plow, making prairie agriculture possible, farmers believed farms would last for generations, providing a stable economy for their descendants: after all, everybody needed food. Most settlers believed, like the author's father and grandfather, "The whole nation depends on the farmer for food." They did not realize how food production would change.

Having an eighty-acre farm represented a dream to those settling the prairie. With several parents and children to operate the farm and provide a living, families also had a promise of shipping the surplus via railroads that had arrived on the plains. Making a living in those days usually meant just that: it didn't necessarily mean becoming rich. Towns and villages sprang up to fill ancillary needs of the farmers. Enrichment of life followed, as traveling lecturers and entertainment troupes arrived to bring culture to this developing part of the country. Andrew Carnegie helped this effort by providing money for libraries in many communities. Peabody, Kansas, one of the small towns in this story, had the first Carnegie library in Kansas. It is alive and functioning today.

Like the tide of the oceans, the surge of population arrived, peaked, and then began to recede. Unforeseen by the residents of the prairie, the strong way of life they developed and knew began to ebb: the eternal principle of change was still at work. This way of life is still working today, 120 years after Andrew Larsen arrived in Marion County, Kansas.

The Prairie Tides relates many struggles, feelings, frustrations, and some of the successes of those living during changes that affected the Midwest. The author has used anecdotes passed along by family members, stories told by neighbors, and personal memories.

This book represents a microcosm of changes affecting the vast Midwest, yes, even beyond the borders of the Jayhawk State and Catlin Township. Rather than being a technically correct history, it contains the recollections of an elderly man, told much as other elders relate tribal histories as they sit with children in jungle clearings or the shadows of canyon cliffs. Other elders will have their own variations to weave into the threads of the past.

The Prairie Tides is set in central Kansas, however, the dreams, actions and accomplishments presented could have been in the Canadian Prairie Provinces or a dozen American states with no great differences. Change is a universal factor in nature and life.

Author's Statement

History is often lost in this age as families mature and children take on responsibilities in other parts of the country. The pioneer's attachment to the land and the stories of the past stretch thin, break, and are often forgotten. Yet when the heritage of land and family is preserved with care, its presentation can be of interest to many. My telling of the maturing of Marion County and my grandfather will vary from others' memories and notes. As more and more notes from various memories are collected, the richness of the past becomes clearer.

Change is always present in our lives. *The Prairie Tides* tells how the central Kansas plains changed from a sea of waving prairie grass to an expanse of tilled land with thousands of rural citizens. Change continued for decades, but population waves crested by the mid-1900s. An ebb tide developed, negating much of the earlier change and progress.

In eras past, families remained in close proximity for years, so events occurring in the past were told, retold, and remembered at family gatherings. With the advent of freeways, moving vans, and jobs in greener pastures in other states, the continuity of traditions eroded and faded. *The Prairie Tides* helps preserve a bit of the richness of bygone years as well as observing the ever-ongoing changes.

The author remembers Grandma Winkley and the "Round Robin" letter she and her female relatives in other states shared. Each lady had a letter in the envelope. When this batch of letters arrived in someone's mailbox, the recipient removed the previous letter she had written, read the rest, and wrote an updating letter before sending the collection to the next relative. When her family gathered for Sunday and holiday dinners, the lady would share what was happening to relatives in areas afar. Long distance telephones calls were limited to bad news, such as deaths and accidents. Family ties were kept close and tight mainly by the three-cent stamp.

The women would share other happenings as they did the dishes after the noon meal. The men would go around the barn to look at the host's livestock and share what had happened in their neighborhoods. Church socials, quilting sessions, ladies' helping-hand clubs, threshing rings, and other shared work and social activities helped develop and preserve a community heritage as well. This is how people kept up with local news. The co-mingling potential of families seldom occurs today other than at winter and spring celebrations: Thanksgiving, Christmas and Easter.

Just as the sea is the most important part of the universe to a sailor, the soil was most important to Grandpa Andy and my father Louis. Let me share some of my heritage with you.

The lives of settlers who brought the first changes are revealed through anecdotes and memories. They are part of the author's family history and heritage.

Part One
Rural Changes

Not just the Indian, but the big bluestem and the buffalo grass
Were to see the radical changes that were to come to pass.
The settlers bought the land, fenced it with a will to keep
It for livestock: horses, cattle, hogs, and sheep.

They settled with children, relatives, chickens, and dreams
While they hitched up their oxen and horses into teams.
Men broke the prairie, harrowed it fine to plant grain,
Then bowed their heads and prayed for rain.

Families and stock increased, but only for a spell.
Meanwhile they built schools, churches, and dug their well.
They had lectures, party phone lines, and later a Model T
Before things eventually began to slip, as we shall see.

Decades later, economies changed, a migration began, a pity.
Jobs were better, it seemed, and the kids went to the city.
But let's remember the way it was and varnish those days
With the pleasure of favorite stories and a little glaze.

Chapter 1

Andy the Runaway

"You'll Never Catch Me!"

"Andy, Andy," the old king shouted,
"Your birthday is getting near."
"I won't go, I won't go," Andy pouted,
And he pretended not to hear.

A ndy Larsen was to become a runaway! The stiff-backed little sheriff warned him in his most authoritative manner, "Don't you do it, Andy. Don't sail to America! Our good king needs you in his army."

"You can't do anything to stop me. The way I have it planned, you'll never see me after Friday! Ever!"

"Well, I'll write your name on my WANTED board, and I'll have you when you come back!" the sheriff assured Andy. "I mean it, Andrew!"

Sure enough, Andy left Odense on Friday and was gone. Odense was a small town on the isle of Fyn, Denmark. It was also Hans Christian Andersen's hometown. While both men were concerned with birds, there is no family record that they knew each other. Since the town was small, perhaps the two had met near a pond or lake. Hans died in 1875, seven years before Grandpa left. While Hans wrote fairy tales about ugly ducklings and swans to become known worldwide as an author, little Andy was minding geese as a goose-herd.

It was 1882, and Andy left before his twentieth birthday to avoid four years of conscription in the king's army. He was a serious youth and saw military duty as a waste of time. His exit set him free, but as we will see, the sheriff was as good as his word: he wrote the name Andy Larsen on his WANTED board probably in large, black, block letters. Perhaps he used an underline or two.

Scandinavian lineage practices are interesting. Andy's father's name was Sorensen. Sorensen's first name was Lars; hence his son's name was Lars's son, Larson. The Danes change the O to an E, hence the spelling, Larsen. This makes tracing ancestors rather challenging. Andy's sister Maggie was Margot Sorensen until she married.

When Andy was old enough his father, a tailor, said to the aging village miller, "Sven, I have taken my oldest boy as my apprentice and I cannot use two. Can my Andy be an apprentice in your mill?" This was one of the flourmills driven by wind-powered sails. The windmills used by the Danes were similar to those of Holland. There was agreement and the miller took Andy as his trainee.

After teaching him how to do most of the menial tasks inside the mill, one morning Sven said, "Andy, come outside. You need to learn how to take a sail and fasten it to the arms so we can start the mill. I'm getting too old for that stuff, and that is why we millers hire you young fellows. Folks your age don't have arthritis yet. When you have mastered setting sail, I will teach you how to take in the sails."

Years later, Grandpa Andy would tell of catching one of the big fan arms and riding it around. He had a jump on the joys of the Ferris wheel, which was invented twenty years later. Imagine being paid for the fun he had riding the mill's fans.

This might be a thrill on a nice day, but visitors would get a different answer when they asked the aged man, "Andy, what about setting sails in bad weather? Was it like taking in the sails of a ship in all types of weather: hot sun, snow, rain, and strong winds?

"Hit vasn't eny fun in badt veather!" Andy's Danish diction flooded into his English and left him, like many first-generation Americans, with an accent. "Hit tuk strong 'ands, a goot sense of balance, and you ditn't let fingernails grow or you voud tear dem."

One of his favorite topics to share with visitors who came to see him in his elder years was the tale of how a miller tested the mill's product. Leaning back in his chair with his head tilted back, Grandpa would raise his chin to one side and partially close his eyes. He closed his index and next two fingers until they touched. Next he rubbed the ends of these fingers with his thumb. "Dat err de vey de miller tests 'is flour, by feeling and smelling," and he raised his fingers to his nostrils to demonstrate the smell test. Licking his forefinger and raising it to the wind, he would continue, "De miller alveys neeted to know vere de vind vas so ee had de sails right. End ee neeted to know dat de machinery was verking right inside de mill," as he cupped a hand to an ear and tilted his head as if listening. In his declining years he enjoyed taking a visitor back to the days of his youth, to share fond memories, and to grind a sack or two of grain with them. His eyes filled with an unusual brightness as his memories came tumbling to the surface.

Grandpa seldom appeared to be a happy person. In fact, he was negative much of the time. But let company come and Grandpa was on his best behavior, especially if they talked to him. It was when he went back seventy years later to mill a sack of grain for his audience that he was at his best. His eyes shone brighter and the usual scowl was replaced with a mellow smile. As a young boy, I not only noticed this transformation of my grandfather, I was fascinated and knew to expect it. If he didn't know a visitor or salesman who was talking to Dad, Grandpa's head would tip forward and his eyes would narrow. The next scripted action was the tightening of jaws and lips. The final part of this role was a shaking of the head.

We don't know his personality or behavior when he left Denmark, other than that he set out with a will and with what few clothes he had. Andy boarded a boat to America, the land of promise. His drive never faded or waned. Succeed he must; he had burned the bridge behind himself. Would the sheriff wait for Andy, a marked man? Though short in stature, Andy walked straight with his head held high and his chin thrust ahead, a habit he continued throughout his life. He was a proud little Dane, like several others I came to know.

He became a driven young man who decided not to have interests other than to succeed with farming. The one exception was Sunday morning at church. When reasonable success arrived, he did not relax a bit. If anything, he became even more intent on achieving further success. When he retired from active farming, he became a lonely person as he had not developed outside interests. His last thirty years were not interesting to him or those around him.

One day short of their fiftieth anniversary, on Sunday, December

7, 1941, my mother, Grace, held a celebration for grandpa and grandma. There was a house full of guests and as mother went to the kitchen for more dessert, she heard the news about Pearl Harbor. She didn't tell anyone until the guests departed. Nettie was not well and left after the gathering to live with daughter Nancy for two more years. Andy who was not much stronger, stayed with us until he died years later.

His daughter-in-law Grace, my mother, would listen to the radio as she did her housework. After someone on the radio made a statement, Grandpa would snort, "Dat feller don't know vat ee's talking bout! Let him batch on de prairie avile vit'out a vife and he'll get schmart in a 'urry!" He seldom heard anything on the radio that related to his two interests: farming or saving money.

Andy lived until he was ninety-two, so he had a lot of lonesome years singing, "Ta, ta, ta ita ta, tee, tee, ta, ta," to himself as he went about picking up little twigs for kindling for our several wood stoves. He was paying dearly for his success. He became a lonely man with a lot of empty time on his hands.

It was common and expected for the elderly to live with their children in later life. His sister, Maggie, would stay with her son Frank for a month or so before going to live with another son, Harry. The grandparents found ways to be useful and there was a bonding with the grandchildren. A strong sense of family developed that does not often happen in the present generation with the advent of retirement and care homes.

The miller's apprentice left home, but could he learn to farm? Would herding geese help him herd cattle and hogs? Would he sink or swim in a sea of grass?

Chapter 2

The Runaway Grows Roots

It's Tough Starting

Plant a hedge, build a home
On the flats where buffalo roam.
Break the sod, plant some grain,
Look heavenward and pray for rain.

To encourage the building of railroads to the West Coast, Congress gave the railroad companies sections of land in a checkerboard fashion ending six miles on each side of proposed routes. In poorer areas the boundary was twelve miles on each side. One legend states the Atchison, Topeka, and Santa Fe Railroad was given twenty-three sections north of the track in Marion County. The same source relates that more than one-third of the county was owned by the Company popularly known as the Santa Fe Railroad. Midway through the Civil War, Congress amended the law to give twenty miles on either side of the route through central Kansas from Emporia to Kinsley.

The railroads then sold these plots of land to families wanting farms and ranches. The sooner there was produce and livestock to carry, the sooner railroads and their investors would earn money.

John C. Fremont, an early explorer, born a half-century ahead of Grandpa, had returned to the East Coast from exploring part of the unknown western lands in the early 1840s. He claimed the central part of the nation was "The Great American Desert." People wondered if the land sale by the railroads might be an uphill task.

In places the Santa Fe Railroad all but followed the Santa Fe Trail. The track reached Peabody and Newton in 1871, eleven years before

Andy arrived. The railroad was soon ready for business.

Pamphlets were printed in many languages by railroad companies and taken to Canada and abroad. This was happening just as the Mennonites, a religious group from Germany, were ending a one-hundred year conscription-free period in Russia that had been granted by Catherine the Great. The purpose of her grant was to draw these people, who were known to be good farmers, to her country. At the time when the grant was issued, Russian peasants were not producing enough food to feed their nation's population. But now the grant was due to expire, and the Mennonites preferred to leave Russia rather than face conscription.

The American railroads knew this, and also knew the Mennonites' reputation for excellent food production. One pamphlet the railroad sales people carried had the message that the Kansas Legislature had decreed that men who belonged to non-resistance religious groups were exempt from military service. This was what the Mennonites needed.

The Santa Fe railroad land agent all but gave these Germans free land to settle on the Kansas prairie. As a productive people, they would grow farm produce that would be shipped via the Santa Fe. The railroad sent a Red Star ship to the Black Sea to bring them to the East Coast. Passage for their farm implements and household goods was free. About 5,000 of these Mennonites made the trip to America, and 3,300 settled in Marion County. Andy must have seen one of the Kansas conscription-free pamphlets, as he arrived in the same era, in 1882. Many of the Mennonite farmers became his neighbors. The Dane had settled in a German neighborhood. He would explain this situation differently. "Dem dern Jermans fight among demselves like cats un dogs, but let dis old Dane come 'round and dey stick together like a bunch of cockleburrs."

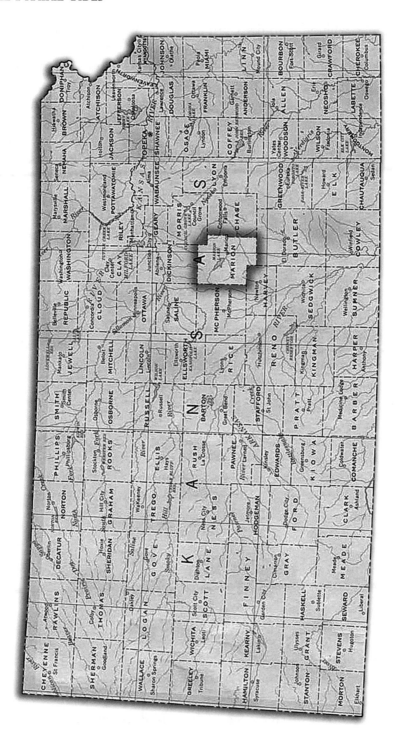

Other religious groups were leaving Russia, as the government became more restrictive. The Russian government saw this and relaxed many of the rules, but many of the country's best farmers were fleeing.

French and Irish pioneers settled six miles east of Andy and started a town, called Florence, on the Santa Fe railroad. Florence had one of the first opera houses in the state. It also had a Fred Harvey House for the Santa Fe passengers. When the trains stopped at Florence, passengers would get off the train to be fed in the Harvey House. Later, when dining cars were added to trains, there was no longer need for the famous Harvey Girls. These young ladies were hired to be the waitresses. They had to be single, of good character, and promise not to marry for a number of months. The hotel and dining room became non-essential and this bit of color disappeared from travel through Marion County. This building remains as a part of local history.

Bohemians from Eastern Europe settled the northern part of the county. Germans were in the center of the county, French and some Irish in the eastern hills. Several Scandinavians, including Andy, together with some English, completed the aggregate. The central plains became an example of the melting pot that America claimed to be.

The first settlers lived in the wind shadow of upturned wagons or whatever shelters they could improvise quickly while they made dugouts or sod houses. The winds came over the prairies from the Western Territories and at times were unrelenting. Other times, as in August, there was no wind and the season of "dog days" became a different problem.

In my youth, my father would often say, "If you don't like the weather, stick around for fifteen minutes for a change." Sometimes, he was correct.

One German settler took his plow and plowed a furrow south from the one Mennonite settlement called Hillsboro across eight or ten miles of prairie to Peabody and the Santa Fe railroad. This was so people wouldn't get lost coming home across the prairie from an occasional visit to Peabody and the Santa Fe. In time a pair of ruts paralleled the furrow before country roads were created.

The process of change was beginning as homesteads became

established. The incoming tide of population and improvement had established itself. *The Standard Atlas of Marion County, Kansas*, by George Ogle and Company, published in 1921, shows many large two-story houses as if they were quite common. A lot of change had occurred in just a third of a century.

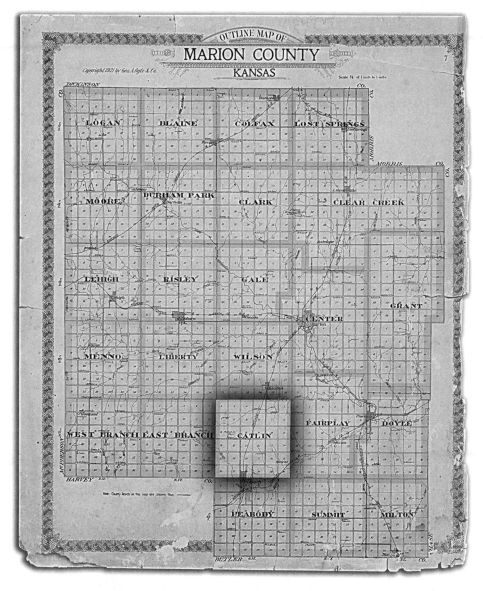

Marion County in 1921.

The first western boundary of both Kansas and Marion County was the Continental Divide in the center of the Rocky Mountains. The Kansas Legislature, not wanting to deal with mining laws, later withdrew the state boundary to the east. By 1882, the year Andy arrived, the county's boundary had stabilized to its present shape, size, and location, north of Wichita and between the wheat belt and the grassy Flint Hills.

The county that year still contained a lot of rolling prairie. There were few trees other than those that grew along creeks or a few cottonwoods growing along a little slough: a vast difference from Andy's crowded homeland.

He arrived by train in Marion and was met with a "Hi Andy" by a cousin named Andersen, who must have been an Ander Somebody's son, hence the last name, Andersen.

"Wait in the wagon, Andrew, as I need to buy some supplies in this store," Andersen said as he handed Andy the reins to the horses and sprang from his box wagon.

Andy noticed a bad odor coming from a barrel outside the store. It was something strong that he had never smelled before. Trying to be helpful, he told his returning cousin, "Eye don't tink you should patronize dat store keeper."

"Why not?"

"Ee 'as a barrel of rottin stuff near 'is door. Can't you schmell hit?"

"That is sauerkraut, a good pickled cabbage," his cousin replied with a broad grin. "There's Germans around here and they love it."

Working as a hired man for his cousin, Andy learned the language and saved his earnings. His wages were fifty cents a day and board and room. He was a frugal fellow who neither drank nor smoked. His son Louis always thought the amount of poverty Andy saw in the Old Country was what created his frugal habits.

The Marion County Board of Commissioners bought a farm two or three miles south west of Marion, near Andersen, on which they built a large hotel-like house along with a set of farm outbuildings. It became known as the Marion County Poor Farm. Going by it was always a reminder that one could have financial trouble even in the Land of Opportunity. Grandpa mentioned "de poor farm" whenever he thought someone was a bit wasteful.

Before long Andy was able to purchase horses and simple farming tools to start a farm of his own in Catlin Township on the southeast corner of section 13. U.S. Highway 50 chose to go by the section and U.S. Highway 77 was located a mile east. Years later they would both relocate several miles away.

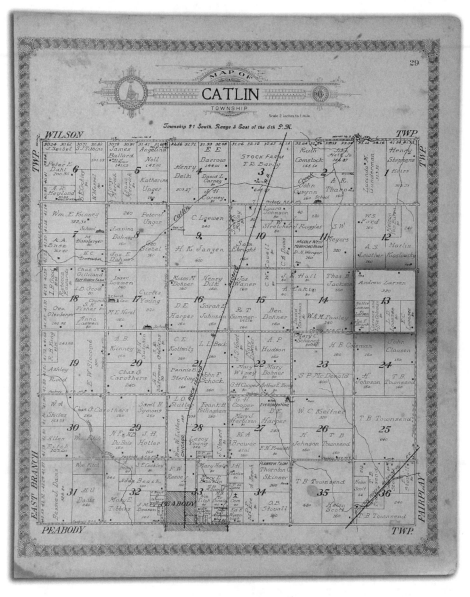

Catlin Township in 1921.

Andy lived the solitary existence of an unmarried man on the prairie – the style of life that became known as batching from the word bachelor. Andy had no enter-tainment except for a cat and dog for evening company, unless the cicadas or coyotes were serenading. A coyote's plaintive song was not comforting and perhaps made the evening even lonelier.

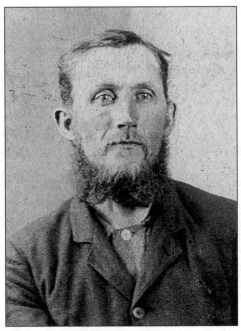

Andy, a new settler.

Years later he told of putting his boots under his cot. "Why did you do that?" he was asked.

"Vel, de boards for de roof dried in de summer sun and shrunk. On clear nights I culd lie in bed un see stars t'rou the cracks. Ven hit rained, water would come in so dat is vy I put my boots under de cot."

Visitors were scarce, and Andy always invited them into his simple home. One visitor staying for a meal was fascinated by how Andy flipped pancakes from the skillet and caught them on the unfried side.

This fellow boldly asked, "Can I try flipping some cakes?" His first try ended with the hot, unfried side falling and wrapping around his wrist, resulting in a horrible burn. He then learned that the batter side doesn't just shake off.

Another time the visitor was an Indian wearing a loincloth hanging in front and at the rear. As it was cold outside, the fellow asked, "Can I warm?" He backed up to Andy's stove to warm himself. As he stood stiff-legged with his legs apart, he swayed back and forth on his toes. His comment, "Feels good," was the last positive statement the fellow made. A cat that was also enjoying the warmth looked up and saw something swinging between the front and back flaps of the loincloth. You guessed it! The cat jumped upward in an attack mode and the poor fellow reacted immediately!

As mentioned earlier, the wind of the Great Plains was with the pioneers much of the time. The settlers from the East knew they needed trees for windbreaks, fence posts, and fuel for their stoves. The Osage orange tree became a top choice: it could live in the harsh climate and its wood provided a very hot fire (although it produced a lot of jumping sparks). The tree branches produced large thorns, which could infect the flesh of anyone unlucky enough to be scratched or punctured.

Osage orange tree trunks cut from the hedgerow became fence posts and locally were known as hedge-posts. Most important, these posts lasted for many years without deteriorating. Once this hard, bright yellow wood had cured it became almost impossible to saw or drive fence steeples into it. Steeple was the word given to the large staple-like pieces of metal used to hold the fence to the posts. (As years passed, the name evolved to staples, although one historian contends that the original word was staple before becoming steeple.)

It was easy to plant an Osage orange hedgerow. The softball-sized, green seed balls were split into sections containing seeds and planted around the farm fields to grow trees that would serve both as a windbreak and as a source of future wood for heating and fence posts. They also provided homes and cover for small birds and animals. Most eighty-acre farms had a hedgerow around them and several cross hedges. The county commissioners passed an ordinance requiring fields to be fenced to keep livestock from straying onto neighbor's land. Thousands of miles of these hedges were planted in central and eastern Kansas as fencing. The state paid farmers $128 per mile of hedge row.

Farther west, trees couldn't get enough moisture to grow well. Without wood for posts, the farmers split sandstone or limestone layers into a post-like shape. Dug into the ground, these stone posts supported the barbed wire for fencing. They have outlasted the Osage orange posts.

Following the Dust Bowl days of the 1930s, the government helped farmers plant trees as windbreaks. Some punster suggested that Roosevelt thought a windbreak across Kansas would keep the wind from reaching Washington.

The census of 1860 counted sixty-four residents in Marion County. The 1870 census showed a population of 768, which swelled to 12,457 in 1880, two years before Andy arrived. The population then grew to nearly 23,000 in 1920. Settlers had become an incoming tide. The vast prairie in Marion County all but became crowded in places where there was better land.

Now, a century later, the rural population has dropped to 8,400 – two-thirds of the 1880 population and only one-third of the 1920 count. Most of the hedges have been eliminated, along with the majority of the farmsteads, clearly an ebb tide. Section 13, where Andy settled, had five houses on it up to the middle of the century. Now only one house is present and it doesn't shelter a farmer.

In the days when the population was swelling, the market grew for hedge seedlings and walking plows to break the prairie. John Deere's improved steel plow allowed a man to develop a farm. Breaking prairie meant following a single plow pulled by a pair of horses guided by the farmer. Early teams were trained to react to verbal commands -- "Gee" and "Haw" causing them to move right or left, just as good sheep dogs respond to whistles for commands. Farmers relished the pungent fragrance of newly turned soil, a very pleasant odor that gave hope for the future.

The farmer would tie the ends of the horse reins into a knot and place the loop over his head to rest upon his neck, as he needed both hands to guide the two-handled, one-furrow plow. One hand could reach a rein to redirect the team, then drop the rein to re-grip the implement if verbal commands had not worked.

Plowing out snakes, including rattlers, was common. Andy wore rubber boots for protection as he walked behind the plow. One day he felt a bite on his heel at each step. His immediate thought: "A rattler, and 'e got Andy!" He stopped, pulled off his boot, and threw it several feet away. As the boot hit the ground, a field mouse jumped out, ran, and hid.

Andy's luck had held this time, but it all but ran out on him later. To earn some extra income, a neighbor named Clausen and Andy took the job of digging the well for the rural Pleasant Hill School, which was then being built. (There would eventually be 137 of these one-room schools in the county; now, at the turn of the twentieth century, there are no rural schools and several towns share instruction responsibilities). It was hard digging the well, as there were plenty of rocks. It was a team effort.

During Andy's turn in the well, he came upon a layer of rock, and called, "'Ey, Clausen, send down a stik ob dynamite und som matches."

Clausen passed the supplies down to him. After getting the dynamite in place, Andy lit the fuse, stepped into the windlass bucket that carried up worker or dirt, and hollered, "All right, Clausen. Crank me up."

No response! Andy yelled louder: "Clausen, de bucket, de bucket. 'Urry!"

Still no Clausen arrived to lift him from the well. Clausen had gone around behind the school to answer a call from nature. He heard Andy and came running with his pants around his ankles. It was a good thing he didn't trip or fall to lose any more time. Just as Andy stepped out of the bucket and onto the ground, the charge went off, throwing the bucket and the windlass into the air before they fell back into the well.

As Andy was telling the story years later, his son Louis, asked, "Why didn't you reach down and pinch out the fuse?"

"I neber tot ob dat!"

How long would Andy batch? Did he continue to live on the prairie? Would he marry and have any children?

Chapter 3

They Wed Anyway
Who Gave the Bride Away?

Nettie kept the ring and they were wed
In spite of what her mother had said.
Nettie had no mother-in-law to give her pains,
That lady was home in the land of the Danes.

Life in his new country continued to give Andy problems. He began courting the English neighbor girl, Nettie Lovesee, on the farm to the west.

Injured at sea, Nettie's English grandfather had immigrated to the Chicago area. The grandfather later left his swampy Illinois land and with his family moved to Kansas, where they would be near relatives and where cheaper land would be available for his sons and himself. Andy's girlfriend told of picking wildflowers as the five covered wagons progressed toward their new home. In 1878 the Lovsees bought the land next to the acreage Andrew would buy four years later.

Nettie had Irish and Welsh ancestry through her mother. When Andy and Nettie began courting, he soon found himself at odds with Mrs. Lovesee although he did not find the full extent of her concerns until later. After he married Nettie, Mrs. Clausen, a Lovesee neighbor, gave the couple a letter written before they married. Andy's children never heard of the episode until the family, dismantling his personal effects after his death, found it.

The one-paragraph, four-page letter was written in beautiful handwriting. The occasional errors in punctuation and capitalization only seem to emphasize Mrs. Lovesee's feelings about Andy.

> *"Grandmother Clausen,*
> *I will never come to see you again you and Lawson are so mean I have been just as good to you and him till this summer. I came over there when you were sick and did all I could for you and manys the cup of good Tea, I have made Lawson and many the dinner I have given him & just see now how he is paying me coming and steal my own dear Child from me and Oh I never needed her so much as I do now and I know you are just helping him do as he does for I heard you had said to him In the spring or fore part of the Summer it doesn't matter one day when he was there you said Annis, why don't you get the ring, get the ring, get the ring Annis and then he goes at it gets her to let him*
> *put it on her finger. Now I think that is just as mean can be. She never came to me. I never thought Lawson would use me so mean after I had been so good to let him have buttermilk & bread and cake some times. We liked him as a friend and neighbor and no more. Oh I think the way he has took to get around Nettie is just awful, awful. Here I am in the morning I can hardly dress myself my hands are so lame I can hardly do anything how long I will be so I don't know and every one says I need Nettie myself and she never would have thought of leaving me if Lawson had let her alone. Now if you don't make him withdraw his suit give Nettie her Liberty. Give Cynthia the ring. she is no relation to him. she would make him a good wife and you would have them both near you and they would make a nice couple she under stands him & he understands her. they are now just the same as Lorenzo & Hattie used to be. just see Colonel Rea & his wife were own Cousins. That doesn't seen right, but second Cousins are no relation to each other. So now this is my mind, I can't help it. you can think it over & let me know. I haven't been deceitful I have always felt friendly towards you all Till Larson began to come & steal Nettie from, me. Now in no other way than I have spoken of can you ever expect me to be your Friend again I would like to be friendly with everybody.*
> *Mrs. R. Lovesee*

The Lovesees, Nettie's parents.

Mrs. Clausen ignored the letter, and Nettie became Mrs. Andy Larsen on December 8, 1891. I wonder about her mother's part in the wedding. Apparently family relations worked themselves out, as finding this letter after Andy's death took his son Louis by surprise. The son had no hint of hard feelings between the two families.

Nettie had gone to Normal School in Marion, the county seat, to get her teaching credential. The first Normal School was a four-week course and that was all. She chose this rather than enrolling in the high school that opened six miles to the southwest in Peabody in 1871. She could soon be teaching and earning a salary quicker by skipping high school. "Who knew what good high school would do for a girl in those days?" was her reasoning. Like her husband-to-be, she was not interested in the social life or activities of the growing towns.

"Andy," she said, after they were married, "you need to learn to read and write English. Sit down and I'll start teaching you." He became fluent in his new language, though he took a short cut now and then. He also was good at keeping accounts. The arithmetic he had learned in Odense served him well. His thriftiness paid off, and he soon had money accumulated to loan to neighbors after he had purchased his several farms.

Andy and Nettie went to church together in the early years, but she didn't attend in her later life. When he was in his seventies, Grandpa would walk the mile to our house to go with us. After church, we dropped him off at his home and visited with Grandma.

Nettie and Andy never had electricity or refrigeration, even in the middle of the twentieth century. Their home life was still much as it had been when they set up housekeeping. During her fifty years of marriage, Nettie cooked and heated her house with wood, a rare commodity on the prairie before all the hedge trees matured.

She dried corn and beans, and stored their potatoes in the cellar, a covered, below-ground room that provided a refuge when a tornado came along. To keep milk from souring, she poured it into a small bucket and hung it with a rope in the well. Cream for butter was skimmed with a spoon off milk that had cooled for several hours. The milk cow's calf became their only meat, except for an occasional rabbit the dog caught. The dog was fed the damaged part and Grandpa and she ate the rest.

Since Nettie bobbed her own hair, she had no reason to visit a beauty parlor. She sewed their clothes and they raised their own food. Trips to town were seldom needed. This saving was another means of not losing one's money and having to go the poor farm.

Nettie loved to read, which in her case was a dangerous practice. She had only a kerosene lamp and would fall asleep while reading a newspaper beside the lamp. The family was always afraid she would knock the lamp over and set the house afire. This happened to her sister-in-law as we shall soon see.

In their later life, Nettie and Andy chose not to have the expense of a party-line telephone to call for help in an emergency. This was rather miserly, since they were probably the wealthiest couple in the township. But it was typical of their reasoning: they didn't need the phone and they would have to buy a pair of batteries for it once or twice a year. Remember the poor farm?

Nettie, Andy and Grandchild, Don.

Their frugality never eased over the years. Buying cheese one day, Grandpa asked, "You got eny Limburger?"

"Yeah, but I won't sell it to you. It's got bugs!"

"Vell, I'll bi som Longhorn and you kin giff me de Limburg' fer free. I kin git rid of it as vell as you kin." (How could spoiling Limburger smell better than the sauerkraut he fussed about after getting off the train in Marion, his first day in the county? Without refrigeration, both storekeepers had a similar problem).

When he came in the house, Nettie saw or smelled the Limburger. She asserted herself. "Out with the Limburger. It doesn't belong in the kitchen with those skippers flying around it. Out!" Andy took the cheese to the smokehouse and would stop to cut off a piece now and then, scraping the skippers off with his knife blade.

This same line of thriftiness continued after Nettie died and Andy lived with us. After eating the pulp from a grapefruit, he would pull the membranes out of the rind and eat them, also. We doubted if he liked them; it probably was to avoid wasting food and running the risk of going to the poorfarm.

Nettie had a brother, Clyde, who was also frugal with money, but perhaps more so with energy. Several stories about him have survived.

One time Andy built a fence one-half mile long between their farms with no help from his brother-in-law. Fence building may look easy, but it involves a lot of hard work: digging postholes by hand, carrying and tamping the posts into the holes, as well as stringing the barbed wire and the driving of steeples (also called staples) to fasten the wire to the posts. As Grandpa was finishing the fence, Clyde arrived and announced, "Andy, you got the fence sixteen feet on my land on the east end."

Andrew shook his head. "My mistake, vhich endt do you vant to start movin hit back vhere it shouldt be?"

Clyde considered the question for a very short time. His lack of energy decided the issue. He concluded that if correcting the error meant he'd have to put in some effort himself, then it didn't matter if the fence remained where Andy had put it.

One very wet fall, Clyde was a little too slow in harvesting his shocked maize. Many of the teepee-like shocks sat in a flooded area of a field. He complained, "The wild geese land on my shocks and take a whole mouthful of grain at a time!" Unfortunately for Clyde, it was a wet winter. He couldn't get a team of horses and a hayrack into the field for months and the geese got all his grain.

Clyde's family looked out for itself. At a church dinner, Clyde's daughter took a plate around the kitchen picking out the family's favorite pieces from all the plates of chicken being set out by others for serving later. One lady, irritated by this, waited until the daughter set her plate of select pieces down and turned her back. Then the alert lady took the plate of chicken and rushed it to the dining room. "Where's our chicken?" the daughter asked when she turned to find her plate of booty missing.

While stories persisted about Clyde and his family, they were gentle, sociable, church-going people. Their way of life did not demand a lot of heavy work or many farm chores. They limited themselves to basic needs and lived within their means. Unfortunately, life had a tragic ending for Jessie, Clyde's wife. One winter morning she backed too close to the open flame kerosene heater and her nightgown caught fire. She died of smoke inhalation.

Andy's and Nettie's first farm home suffered the loss of a roof from a tornado, which also ruined Nettie's parents' house. The same storm destroyed the Pleasant Hill School where Grandpa dug the well with Mr. Clausen's help. An account of the day states that no board longer than three feet was found.

Tornadoes are common in the Midwest. They occur in late spring and early summer as the warm, damp air from the Gulf of Mexico is met by much colder air coming from the north. When clouds build quickly and turn dark or show a lot of dirty greenish tan, it is time to check the horizon and head for shelter. Settlers soon learned about tornadoes and built storm cellars or storm caves as retreats. Indians shared some knowledge including their belief that a tornado never approached a fork in a river or a place where two rivers merged.

Eighty years later another tornado hit Andy's second farm which he had purchased and developed diagonally across the section from his first one. The couple spent most of their life on this second farm. Their great-grandson, Larry Larsen, my son, lived on this farm at the time of this second twister. The house was spared, but all the barns, the outbuildings, and the silo were lost. It appeared that this tornado split into two forces. Besides destroying the farm, it demolished a house across the road and moved a granary off its foundation. Trees between the two houses were not hurt.

Grandpa's barn after the tornado.

By tracking the fallen trees in the hedgerows, Larry could trace the tornado's path across a section or two. Fortunately. His family was not hurt but terribly surprised. A lot of work and time was required to coordinate the claim to the insurance company and the work of a contractor who dug huge trenches to bury the wreckage.

Andy and Nettie moved to their second farm described above in 1899. Eventually he managed to own all four corners of section 13, range three, east. At one time or another he lived in each of the four-houses, the last two while in retirement.

The first house on the second farm was a tiny home, about ten feet by twenty feet. It must have been crowded, in this small building contained not just Andy and Nettie, but also their growing family. Nancy, the couple's first child, was born October 1, 1892. Her brother Bob made his appearance February 7, 1895, also in the tiny house.

The third child made his rapid arrival in due time on July 21, 1900. Nettie told Andy, "Hurry to the Babcocks' and bring Mrs. Babcock quick; this baby's going to arrive soon." Hitching horses to the buggy again, "daddy-to-be" headed eastward to the neighbors' house three-quarters of a mile away. But Nettie birthed the child herself, as Andy and Mrs. Babcock were late in getting there. When they arrived she was holding a boy baby. They tidied up and made her comfortable which was all the help she needed. The baby boy was named Louis Philo Larsen. When he grew up he would become my father. The name Philo came from a relative, Philo Hansen (Hans Somebody's son).

Andy plunged into hog raising on his second farm and succeeded well enough that he was able to build a two-story, five-bedroom house two years later.

The little house that been Dad's birthplace was converted to a shop and a corncob bin.

Corncobs were kept after the corn shelling for use as kindling in the heating and kitchen stoves. The cobs were almost a necessity for starting a quick fire in a stove on a cold winter morning. They caught fire quickly and burned very hot

It was always nice to have a clean cob in a coat pocket when doing winter fieldwork since dead weeds didn't make good toilet tissue. In the outhouse, the women used Wards or Sears catalogues for this purpose. Many boys learned about women's underwear and had their beginning pre-sex education from those catalogues.

Outhouses also had another purpose once a year. They became Halloween targets for the big boys wanting to celebrate the occasion.

Shortly after building the new house, Andy purchased the family's first and only bathtub, ordering it by mail from a Montgomery Ward or Sears Roebuck catalogue. The galvanized tub looked like a portable upright wooden closet as it sat next to a wall. It folded down to hold water for bathing. After Andy and Nettie retired, none of the other houses they lived in had bathrooms or tubs. At that time outhouses or privies were used not only on the farm but also in the little towns.

Andy built a barn that was large by anyone's standards. He also built a long hog house having an overhead grain storage floor. A large drive-through granary completed the main farm buildings. There were several small outbuildings. Nettie didn't need a brooder house to start baby chicks: she started out by using only brood hens to raise her first chickens. She did have the use of a chicken house to care for the hens that produced eggs.

The new barn had stalls for four teams. Eight teams were required for haying. A team was needed for the mowing machine, one for the dump rake, and another for the buck rake-or as it was called locally, a go-devil which was used to buck or bring hay to the stacker from the windrows left by the dump rake. Lastly, a team was needed to operate the hay stacker. Since mowing the hay was the slower of the operations, there may have been another team and mower.

How could this twenty-year-old man arrive in a strange land where he didn't know the language, start as a hired hand in a new occupation, and accomplish so much so quickly? There are several parts to the answer. First, remember he neither drank nor smoked and there were few places nearby for this frugal boy to spend his small wages.

Second, the land was relatively cheap. He did not buy his land from either the Santa Fe railroad or the United States government. He was the third owner according to county records.

Production costs were relatively low. He used horsepower, which had several advantages. The mares could produce another horse each year, so power replacement costs were minimal. The horses helped raise their own fuel, whether hay or oats, and the pasture was ever present.

When Andy was farming there were no gasoline costs, and insurance and legal costs were nil. The family raised most of its food and Nettie and her daughters made some of the clothes at home. Hardware and sometimes seed were bought, as well as some medicines, though often the ointments they used were homegrown or homemade. A lard-and-turpentine mixture was used to help horse scrapes and wounds heal.

Another low expense item was Andy's labor costs. Besides his sons, Louis and Bob, Andy had several hired men most of the time. Labor is usually expensive, but not for Grandpa in his timeframe. Neighbors traded work when needed, especially at threshing time. Andy remembered working while learning English. He encouraged other young Danes arriving to work for him until they had command of the language and could find better jobs working for someone else.

The farmhands' labor wasn't limited to summer work. In the spring the hired men were needed for fixing fence and planting crops. In the fall and winter they helped shuck the fields of corn, haul hay from the haystacks in the fields, feed the cattle and hogs, as well as cut hedge for firewood or fence posts to install or sell. Grandma used a lot of firewood as hot water was needed for washing clothes, cooking, and heating the house in winter.

Andy had one Dane who was a not too sharp. This fellow, Dimmit, liked to cut hedge year around. As there were no power saws in those days, each tree had to be felled with an axe before it could be processed as a post or firewood.

Dad tells of sneaking down the hedgerow as a young boy, too young for fieldwork, to spy on Dimmit. Louis liked to listen to this fellow at work. Raising a fist to the tree he was about to fell, the fellow would address it. "You's a bash one!" He might then quote some Bible verse before continuing, "but I'll get ya, you sinner! Judgment time's cummin'"

One day, a tree rolled as it fell, pinning the woodsman to the ground. At that point, Louis made his presence known and went to help the downed man free himself. "Touldn't help it. Touldn't help atol!" was the poor man's comment.

"Now dat ve 'avf a family of tre kits, a goot farm, and a new 'ouse, I'd like to show you and de kids to my foks," Andy told Nettie. "Ve'll go vhen de 'arvest ist in. Ve'll neet some sootcases."

When the alert Marion County sheriff heard about the impending trip, he asked, "Andy, did you ever get your citizenship papers?"

"Noo. Vhy?"

"I heard you skipped out of Denmark with the sheriff after you. They might still be mad at you for that. You'd better get yourself processed!"

Grandpa did and put his citizenship papers in his pocket. Sure enough, the Danish sheriff was waiting for him at the foot of the gangplank. Stepping forward from the waiting greeters, the sheriff waved his arrest warrant and flashed a big smile of satisfaction, saying, "I got you this time, Andy!"

"Doo kin play dat game," Andy said as he held up his crisp, new citizenship papers. "Goot morning and gootbye." He walked on, leading his brood with his head held high.

The three Larsen children played and slept with cousins and learned to speak some Danish before returning home with their parents. Louis celebrated his sixth birthday in Denmark.

The family returned to Catlin Township, northeast of Peabody and took up life where they left it earlier. The runaway was well rooted in his new land.

Would Andy's fortune be as good in the future? Would there be more children? One wonders if his dialect will ever be overcome. The early part of the twentieth century was full of change and it might continue.

Chapter 4

A Toe is Lost

Boys Were Boys, Decades Ago

Louis lost his toe on the way to school.
The accident was absolutely silly.
Wait till you hear his brand-new rule:
Don't run barefoot near a trotting filly.

The Larsens returned to the farm as a happy family. Andy had not been detained. His children had met a new set of cousins and grandparents while Nettie met her in-laws for the first and only time. Once back, they immediately returned to the farm routine.

The kids were going to school in the buggy on a rainy day. Louis kicked off his shoes to run barefoot in the mud beside the pony. Running this close was to bring him grief. He took one step too near the pony and a hoof came down upon his toes. Half of his middle toe was severed but the other toes were not damaged.

Despite the mishap, Louis liked ponies. Even before becoming old enough to work in the fields, he enjoyed riding into a nearby slough to pick mulberries from the trees while sitting astride his pony.

A mulberry tree on the farm was a delight for birds and kids alike. These inch-long, pencil-sized berries, cooked with rhubarb and pineapple, made a great jam or pie. Little stems were ignored and served as roughage, or what we now call fiber. Today, stems would be considered a contaminant: we would throw them away and take a roughage pill.

The reason so many trees of this species were planted near Peabody was to provide ample leaves for the worms in the silk factory located north of town, which produced quality silk cloth for only two years. As schoolchildren we learned that Japanese silk worms were fed the leaves of the mulberry tree. Their Kansas cousins needed the same diet. Many farms near town had a number of such trees. However, I never heard Dad or Grandpa tell of the local collection of leaves.

Louis's dog, Tige, was his constant companion. If a hog got out of the pen, the cry, "Here, Tige! Here, Tige!" not only brought Tige on the run but also caused the hog to quickly find its way back into its pen. The hog remembered the last time he was outside his pen. Tige had grabbed an ear with a toothy mouth and jerked.

Louis heard Tige barking one day along a hedge and went to investigate. Nettie raised a few guinea fowl, and a bull snake had discovered a nest. The snake had helped itself and was bumpy with the eggs it had swallowed. The snake held Tige at bay momentarily with a frightening posture and a lot of hissing. Then Tige made his move. He grabbed the snake by the middle and shook it violently from side to side. The eggs in the front half of the snake went flying.

Snakes find eggs a great diet. Mrs. Hett, a neighbor, while gathering eggs, found the rear end of a snake extending from a knothole over a hen's nest. An egg bulge prevented the snake from sliding the rest of the way through the knothole. When she went to the other side of the wall, the front half of the snake was dangling above another nest. There was another egg bump on that side of the knothole, preventing the snake from backing through the hole to escape. It was trapped until it could digest one egg or the other.

Dad liked turnips and near the first of July he made it a point to buy turnip seed in bulk to sow on his birthday. "Sow your turnips on the twenty-first of July, wet or dry," he would say. One of his jobs as a boy was to take his little red wagon to a turnip field and bring back a wagonload of the roots to feed Andy's hogs. Dad's taste for turnips never diminished.

Louis's younger sister, Evie, short for Evelyn, was born the January after they returned from their trip. Perhaps she was nicknamed Evie because she didn't like her first name, Fannie.

As a boy, my dad had a lot of fun teasing Evie. After supper she would run to the cot by the wall. He would run over, pull the cot from the wall and push her off. Then he would shove the cot over her and lie on it himself. He was a teaser throughout his life, shifting his targets to sheep, the dog, or turkeys once Evie was grown and gone.

His mischief was not limited to home. He would laugh as he told of one prank. "I found some tobacco on the way to school," he said. "Everyone, including the teacher, was playing ball in Ruggles's pasture across the road from the one-room school. I put the tobacco on the heating stove and joined the game. By the time classes were to start, the room smelled very strong of burnt tobacco. The windows had to be opened, and we got to play another inning of ball while the school was aired out."

A decade later one of the Dunn boys trapped a skunk, removed the odor gland, and threw the gland into Marion high school's internal ventilating fan before school. The horrible smell filled the whole building. The culprit was caught, and although school was dismissed for the rest of the student body, he was caught and kept in school all day.

"At school, we boys played the game Shinny," Dad told his children years later. "It was like hockey except the puck was a flattened tin can. One fellow always had the advantage. I found a hedge limb shaped correctly and converted it into a new stick. Since hedge sticks were all but unbreakable, I was going to fix that guy! When I squared off with him and the puck was dropped, I just pushed the hedge stick into the ground and held on. Sure enough, the guy who was so quick swung, and when his stick hit my hedge stick, his broke." At that point in the story telling, Dad dropped his head to one side, barely repressing a pleased smile.

In the early decades of the century some of the schoolboys were really young men. They were in their upper teens by the time they reached the end of the eighth grade. For them, school didn't start in the autumn until the fall crops were harvested, and they dropped out in the spring when the ground could be worked and crop planting started.

Andrew built a stone smokehouse for curing meat after butchering. A large cottonwood tree stood beside it. Louis told of being in the tree with a machete-like corn knife one day when Dimmit, the not-to-sharp hired man, walked by. "I dropped the knife. It hit the roof and scooted off, landing just in front of the fellow. Dimmit reared back and looked and looked until he saw me. He tried to climb the tree with no results. He kept sliding back to the ground."

Louis laughed as he told the story years later. "The guy told Dad about me. 'Dat 'boise ish a bad 'un.' Dimmit said. 'E tried to till me!'"

Louis didn't smoke, but his older brother, Bob, started using a pipe on the sly. Sometimes when Bob hid the pipe away before supper, it would be smoked out when he returned to it later. Bob decided to put a stop to this. He went to the chicken house and all but filled the pipe from the droppings he found under the roosts. He then put some tobacco on the top and singed the tobacco before going to supper. After supper the hired man told Bob, "You need to get some different tobacco, Bob. That tastes like chicken _____!"

"That's what it was," Bob said. The hired man lost his supper and Bob never had any pipe trouble again.

Andrew found out about the smoking and announced, "I don't vant you poises to smoke. Hif you don't smoke before you ere tventy-vone, I'll giv you one'undred dollars on your birt'day." That represented a lot of money to a boy in those days. Bob didn't get his, but Louis collected.

The oldest sister, Nancy, was a neat lady. She taught school for several years before she let Will McGinness court her. Coming home from courting her one night, Bill, as he was called, went to sleep. Never mind, the horse knew the way. However, the horse pulled up close beside the barn and our Uncle Bill-to-be couldn't get out on his side of the buggy.

Nancy soon changed her name to Mrs. Will McGinness. She wore her hair bobbed and dressed rather plainly. She loved children and referred to them as "little fellers." When she came out of church at Aulne, the small town three miles north of the farm, children would rush to her to say hi, tell her a story, or put their arms around her. When people came to her house to visit, she had a cookie for them. She would find her latest *National Geographic* magazine and show the children something she thought they would like to see. Other times she would take them into her kitchen and show them a lemon growing on a tree she grew from a seed in a pot on her kitchen windowsill. It was always fun to go to her house.

Nancy's youngest boy, Ed, was in college when my girlfriend Jacquie Hawbecker, a Marion girl, and I were at Kansas State College (now Kansas State University). One January, the three of us headed for the campus, eighty miles away in Manhattan. It was a windless, full-moon night, and very cold. It had snowed, but the roads had been cleared. We started the two-hour ride after evening church. North of Herington, Ed's Model A began to act sluggishly. We crept along more slowly by the mile. "The muffler might be the problem," Ed decided. "I'll backfire and see if that helps." As we started down a long hill he cut the ignition, filling the muffler with gas fumes. At the bottom of the hill he said, "Here goes," as he turned the ignition on. There was a tremendous report that probably frightened sleeping crows from their perches in half the township.

The speed increased immediately, but there was a scraping noise. "Sounds like the tailpipe is dragging," one of the group said. Ed coasted to a stop and cut a piece of wire from some farmer's fence to hold the tailpipe off the pavement.

We roared through that hushed valley. As we came to Junction City and Manhattan at last, Ed slowed to an idle and he crept to the apartments with a hoarse chuckle, chuckle from the Model A.

We were lucky we had plenty of clothing that night. The morning paper reported the temperature had dropped to twenty-seven below zero just as we arrived!

Uncle Bob, the fellow with the chicken-manure pipe, had a mind of his own. After coming home from France and World War One, he farmed for a year or two without much success, then headed to the California oil fields. He, too, was a colorful individual according to family stories.

Evelyn, the last of the four children, also taught school and ended up several counties west of home. There she met Roy Grybowski. He flew a plane and would fly down to court her during the summer. If on a Sunday morning my family saw a plane in a neighbor's pasture, we knew Roy and Evie would be seen in church.

They were married in the early 1930s and stayed with Andrew and Nettie for several months while Roy tried farming. In those times, a shivaree several nights after the wedding was custom. Noise started the ritual. Tricks followed: short sheeting the couple's bed or putting cornflakes between the sheets was typical, together with any creative, extemporaneous idea that presented itself, such as hiding shoes and removing labels from cans of tinned food. On this night, neighborhood boys knew about Nettie's nest eggs, those marked and left in a nest to coax a hen into using it rather than going somewhere else to lay her egg. These marked eggs were old and rotten. The boys gathered them with a flashlight and placed them in Evie and Roy's bed.

Roy was no more successful at farming than Bob, so he and Evie also went to California. After sleeping on a park bench for several nights, Roy got a job and later had his own business, selling and repairing motor scooters as well as TVs. He was every bit as frugal as Andrew and before long had a beautiful home on the hill overlooking Santa Barbara.

Roy loved to talk about flying if he had an audience. One interesting story concerned his wanting to see his son on the island of Puerto Rico without buying a flight ticket. He and a friend found someone who wanted a plane delivered to Puerto Rico, so Roy offered to fly it at no cost. "We ran into clouds and fog east of Florida. As a fly-by-the-seat-of-my-pants pilot with no instrument ratings, I wondered how I was doing. I dropped a quarter to see if it would fall to the floor or the ceiling of the plane. We made it OK."

Before marrying, Roy delivered oil-field parts by air. He set down successfully into one oil field but had problems getting out. The tall wooden derricks and a farmstead didn't offer him much room to become airborne. He pulled the tail of his plane back between two derricks and gunned the motor. "When I landed I found some of the farmer's windmill caught on the plane," he insisted.

The longer the audience remained, the better the stories became. Everyone looked forward to listening to Uncle Roy. Aunt Evie would listen to him in a quiet manner with a smile on her face. I often wondered about the true meaning of that smile.

With two children in California, would Andy spend winters there? What would happen on the farm without Bob and Roy to help? Would Louis stay in Catlin Township? Would he be allowed to take over the farm?

Chapter 5

Serious Farming

The Farmer Couldn't Do It Alone

The hired hand came and made a stand
To work wherever he was needed.
He grabbed a tool and lent a hand
To plow the land, harrow, and seed it.

Returning from Denmark in 1906, Andy brought several big Danish boys back with him. These fellows also wanted a start in America, and they needed to learn the language for this to happen. They worked for not much more than room and board. After a year or so they had learned English and would strike out on their own as Andy had done. One young Dane, Hans Madsen, was stubborn and announced, "If dey vant to talk to me, dey kin learn Dansk." As a result he worked as a hired man for the rest of his life, stumbling along with crippled English. He never broke into the growing mainstream of upward movement so common to the many immigrants who were to make the country strong.

Hired men were a necessity if an early farmer was to be successful. This is apparent when you remember that the power available to farm the land was only a team of horses and the small implements the team could pull. The farmer's only alternative to hired men was to hang on until he could raise several boys to help. Farming, even on a small acreage, meant a lot of hand work: pitching hay into the barn or haystacks, hauling hay from the stacks to feed animals, shucking corn, shocking grain bundles, threshing, cutting hedge, making fence, and doing daily chores.

The larger farms usually had a hired man or men year around as there was a lot of work in the winter also: cleaning barns, feeding cattle and hogs, cutting hedge, and hauling grain. On small farms there was a seasonal peak for extra summer help. A lot of unemployed men in the early part of the twentieth century would drift into the Midwest for a summer job on a farm. They liked working outdoors. The home-cooked food was good: fried chicken, corn on the cob and home baked bread with gravy. In mid-spring these men would be seen walking down the highways, stopping and asking farmers if they needed a "summer hand." This was the era before paperwork invaded the farm: OSHA, workman's comp, overtime pay, liability insurance, and unions.

On haying days, Andy's orders might have been: "Louis and Bob, 'arness up and git de mowers goin vhile de rest ob us do de chores. Vhen ve git to de field, Hans, you and Lars rake and run de buck rake. Ve got to 'urry, as dere ish a cloudbank in de nortvest. Vhen Bill gits here, he and I vill do de stacking."

This meant Grandpa would operate the stacker to place a load of hay on the stack and Bill would arrange the hay when it got there.

"Ve better hurry. Dere's a cloud in de vest," Grandpa would repeat to himself. When the stacker would act up or break and the process stopped, Bill would sit down and sing just loud enough for Grandpa to hear, "Blessed be nothing, blessed be nothing." With the chance of getting the hay wet and Bill singing smart songs on company time, Andy was soon fit to be tied.

Bill was one of a kind. An African American man, he was the Larsens' neighbor to the east. He was a bachelor who did not farm but worked in the community as a hired man, or hired hand, to use the local phrase. Bill could and did easily stir up other folk. For example, he had a telephone with a long receiver cord. He would lie on his cot in the evening and listen to all the conversations on the party line, which angered neighbors.

One spring he went to the annual school board meeting to talk against any spending the board might propose. A board member, who became tired of this, grabbed a poker from the school stove and ran Bill out of the building. Bill ran only until he could retrieve his razor from a pocket, open it, and run the board member back into the schoolhouse.

On rainy days, fieldwork stopped and attention turned to other kinds of work. The men would clean barns, trim decorative hedges, mow weeds, shingle buildings, fix fences, worm hogs, castrate young male animals, shell corn, grind feed, and catch up on items postponed while field work had taken top priority. Another task was to use a drag to knock clods of dirt into road ruts. A newly hired man might think that rain would bring a slight vacation, but he would learn that wet weather merely switched the types of work he would be assigned

Andy's hired hand, Dimmit, was not able to do much other than cut and trim hedge. Since the farms all had hedgerows around them, this could be nearly a full-time job winter and summer. Andrew's morning orders included him also. "Dimmit, still got eny 'edge left to cut?"

"Oh yeth, Mr. Larthen, ah do."

"Vell, I guess you kin go to it. Ve von't neet you haying."

"Thank you, thank you." Grabbing his axe, Dimmit started across a field to the place where he'd left off the night before.

Thirty years later, Dimmit returned to visit the farm and found Dad operating it. Dad, our visitor, and I were milking when we heard an awful howl. Glancing up, Dad and I saw that the cow Dimmit was milking had shifted her stance and was standing on his tennis shoe. Now, anyone who has milked knows to put his or her head into the cow's flank and push to keep her from crowding. She has to shift the rear feet to maintain a balance, and the problem is resolved. The former hired hand had forgotten this. He didn't react, but continued to howl until the cow looked around at him and walked away.

One of Dad's summer hands was a fellow named Henry who returned five years in a row. He was a fascinating man to my sister and me. He wore a lined leather jacket all day long in the summer, regardless of what he was doing. Then on Sunday, while we were at church, he would borrow one of Mother's tubs and wash the jacket at the well. He claimed he kept cool by working up a sweat in the jacket and letting the moisture of the sweat evaporate. He was not a fast worker but he was steady; he never slowed down or took a break. At the end of the day he had kept up with the best of the crew. He was different in another way: he smoked a pipe, but only in the evening. He allowed my sister and I to light ladyfinger firecrackers from it on the Fourth of July.

In 1940s, Dad hired Sam, another fellow who was not very bright. As a young man, a decade or more earlier, this fellow was caught chasing the girls in the city park. He was sent to the institution in Winfield. There he was castrated and sent home to his aging parents. This now docile fellow was a good worker and could handle the remaining team of horses we had on the farm. He cleaned barns, cut hedge, and did about everything except run the tractor. He was very good with animals and their care.

Sam let another worker down only once. He and I were trimming hedge one cold winter morning when I received an urgent call from nature. As I dropped my gloves and unzipped my two pairs of coveralls, I asked, "Sam, watch and let me know if anyone is coming down the road." He forgot. Squatting in front of the brushpile, I looked up and into the startled eyes of Effie Coleman, an elderly neighbor to the south. She was looking out of the window of their quiet car as her husband Clarence drove slowly past us. I had been caught in the "you know what situation." Sam chuckled about that the rest of the morning.

My Jacquie had been pregnant with our daughter Karen several months when Mother remembered a tale she had heard years earlier: it was unwise to have an unusual situation, such as a retarded person, around a mother to be. Would Sam's presence affect her first grandchild? Dad stopped using the fellow as a precaution. (P.S. Karen turned out to be A-OK).

Jacquie and Don ready to settle down.

Some might think it was not "kosher" to use fellows like Dimmit and Sam; however, they were treated and paid the same as other hired men. They felt they measured up to other hands, and they developed a sense of satisfaction. The key was respect rather than exploitation. Sam could stay at home with his parents on weekends, yet feel needed during the week. He had as much fried chicken and ice cream as the members of the family. Often these folks were sent to institutions away from family where they found it hard to have self-worth.

McKinley was another memorable farm worker. He had just passed middle age and was a likable, good worker. This fellow was one of the few bearded men we saw in those days but that is not the reason our family remembered him.

The reason was ice cream. We always had a lot of it and it gave McKinley trouble. In the winter ice was obtained for the freezer by breaking it from the livestock tank. In the summer, whoever went to town for supplies would bring home a block or two of ice, one for the icebox used during harvest and the other for ice cream. After chores and supper were finished we would crank a freezer of ice cream or sherbet. McKinley would take his bowl of the cold dessert fresh from the freezer and gobble it, one spoonful after another. In a few minutes he would be finished. Then he would lean forward, holding his head and moan, "It goes to my head. Oh it hurts!" He never learned to eat the ice cream at a slower rate.

When Mother had the most work she often had a hired girl. Her garden was large. I was perhaps two hundred feet long and fifty feet wide. That amount of garden took a lot of time to plant, cultivate, weed, and harvest. To process the food, whether canned or frozen, took yet more time. The garden was her pride, and she worked hard to be a good provider.

Mother loved to raise and can tomatoes. When the cattle were away on summer pasture, cucumbers grew well below the livestock tank where water leaked; that meant she could put up a lot of pickles. When it was time for the roasting ears to be gathered, she would gather several gunnysacks of them and can corn.

As the fruit season arrived there would be apricots, peaches, cherries and plums to can. Mother's kitchen was extra hot during the summers when it could reach one hundred degrees outdoors. All her canning was done on a wood-fired stove. These were the days before air conditioning.

Besides helping with the canning, the hired girl could help with the washing for the family and the hired man. There were meals to cook and when we had the threshing crew there would be seven to ten extra men for the noon meal and a mid-afternoon lunch.

A routine became standard for the farm. Many of the settlers came to settle the land wanting to own their own property and to make a living. With the help of the hired hands and a diversity of crops and animals, it was possible to make not only a living but also extra income. A savings account could be started.

Would the pace continue? Were changes ahead? If so, what kind, and how soon would they come? Railroads were replacing wagon trains and ox carts. What next?

Chapter 6

The Way They Did It

Animals Were a Must

A birthing sow is said to farrow
A gilt is a young maiden she.
A neutered he is called a barrow,
And a boar is an un-neutered he.

Mother with Dad's first mules.

We seldom think of horses as a crop, but their reproduction was important. Older horses needed to be replaced, and a growing son would be able to operate a second team of horses if they were available. As a farmer's son matured, he would need a team to start his own farming.

If there was a surplus horse, it could be sold to another farmer. Other markets included the people in town: the undertaker, the lumberyard owner, the fire department, and townspeople who had a surrey or buggy.

My wife's grandfather was a horse buyer for the Army, which had a tremendous need for replacement horses. One can imagine the number of horses it took to build the country roads and move dirt for the new railroad track beds being built.

Much of the dirt moving was done with a man, a team of horses, and a dirt slip. The slip could be likened to a horse-drawn dirt scoop. One common slip had a pair of handles that the operator lifted to cause the front edge of the slip to cut dirt from the ground. Pushing down on the handles would stop the cutting/loading process so the load of dirt could be slid to where it was needed. At the place the dirt was to be unloaded, the operator would raise the slip's handles again but somewhat higher. The leading edge of the tool would bite into the earth again since the slip was pulled from a yoke attached to its middle. It would then turn over, thus unloading its load of dirt.

Since the tool was developed in Fresno, California, it was known as a Fresno slip. These slips moved a lot of dirt to develop the irrigation canals, roads, and railroad track beds of the midwestern and western states.

A young colt went to the fields with its mother when the mare was in harness. It ran beside her and was not a problem generally. At threshing time, when dangerous belts ran from the tractor to the threshing machine, the colt was left in the barn, a frightening experience for the colt. At noon the mare was returned to the barn and the colt could have a nursing lunch.

Louis had a colt named Prince, son of Queen, who did not want to be weaned. Louis tried many ways to help Queen wean Prince, to no avail. Prince did not want to give up the nursing habit. Queen tried to avoid his approaches for a milk lunch by moving away and swinging her head in a threatening manner. She started to kick, but he still persisted. The first few times he got a hoof on the head, he might have thought the blow was an accident. Shaking his head, he moved toward Queen again. Then he seemed to have second thoughts as he shook his head and moved away. With a satisfied smile, Louis said, "I think he just gave up the milk diet. He's on his own now."

Now and then, life could become exciting when a farmer had a runaway team of horses. At least three such instances are remembered by the Larsens. Louis had a pair of mares that had only one good eye between them. While he was closing a field gate, something spooked the mares, and they broke into a run for the farmstead. After turning into the driveway, the mare with the good eye veered enough to miss running into the granary, but her partner, the blind one, ran into it at a full gallop. The wagon they were pulling hit her from behind and rammed her farther into the wall. She was not hurt badly, but Dad had to render first aid to both her and the building.

On another occasion, coming home on the narrow dirt road, I had to crowd the wheel of a wide hay rake into the ditch to allow a car to pass. The rake jerked hard enough that the doubletree pin fell out, releasing the horses from the rake. I had to let go of the reins to remain on the rake seat. Hearing the doubletree banging at their heels, the horses got excited and headed home as fast as they could. They didn't quite make the turn into the lane. Instead, they crashed through the little decorative hedge into our front yard. Here they straddled Mother's clothesline and stripped the clothes from it. Galloping past the farmhouse they mangled their way over the backyard fence and crowded into their barn stall. Unhurt, I came home a distant second in the race.

The next summer, I was taking a hayrack north to help some neighbors, the Hetts, fill their silo. I took a sack of cucumbers along for Mrs. Hett and hurried north. Noticing that the cucumber sack was falling over, I bent to control it. In doing so, I slackened the reins, and a buckle on the reins going to both mares slipped through a ring on Queen's collar. Pulling the rein did not return the buckle to a normal position, and thus did not signal the mares to slow. The noise of the steel-wheeled hayrack became louder. The team became excited and ran faster, causing the hayrack to become even noisier. By now both horses were running at top speed. It happened to me again: the doubletree pin bounced out and the mares were free. They headed for Russ Hett's barn a quarter of a mile away. Queen did not make it: Blondie's neck yoke came loose, and Queen stepped on it at a full gallop. She ended up lying on the neck yoke, so she couldn't get up and continue the flight. Blondie found her way into a stall in the barn. By the way, cucumbers were scattered quite a distance.

Louis used mules in the 1930s. Mules did not need as much grain nor as high a grade of feed to stay in good condition as did the horses. He liked the dependability of mules. He could drop the reins in the field and walk home for repairs. The mules would be waiting for him when he returned. He never had a runaway with any of his four mules. He always had to tie horses to something or they would walk or run off.

His black mule, Pete, had very sensitive skin. Louis was always using an ointment or turpentine mixed with melted lard on the irritated spots. If a fly landed on Pete and he could not reach it with his head or tail, this mule would lie down and roll. This caused a lot of harness repairs often on the spot.

Monk, Pete's partner, did not have this problem. One day, as Dad was mowing prairie hay, he mowed over a bumblebee nest. One bee repeatedly stung Monk. She switched her tail with vigor but did not miss a regular step. Since the bee did not attack Pete, his behavior was normal.

Jack and Jenny were a gentle, matched brown pair of mules used when I started fieldwork, somewhere around ten years of age. I cultivated rows of corn with them for several years.

Some mules had an ornery streak. Dad heard a pig squealing bloody murder one day. He ran around the barn, with the dog along for assistance, to locate the problem. Halfway out the lane toward the pasture stood a mule with its eyes closed, holding a pig by the ear in its mouth. The pig was off the ground, gyrating, and squealing at the top of its lungs.

Hogs were another animal that were found on most family farms. They ate a lot of table leftovers and slop. To make the slop, the farmer poured the skim milk that remained after the cream was separated from the milk into a barrel containing several buckets of ground grain. Any household scraps were added before the barrel was filled with water. Later, this soaked-grain-and-milk mix was put into a long hog trough at feeding times. These animals were easy to raise unless they contacted the dreaded disease cholera. One sick pig with cholera and the whole herd became sick or died.

While there were a few purebred breeders around, most farmers chose a breed they liked but they did not keep papers on individual hogs. Like cattlemen buying a purebred bull, they might buy a purebred boar now and then to help keep the line strong with the features of the particular breed. Each breed was known for certain features: large litters, quick growth, good temperament, etc. A hog man might be a Duroc man just as he was a Ford car person, or a farmer with Berkshire hogs would have feelings as strong for them as for his Dodge car. A book about Marion County published in the early 1900s states that Andy Larsen was a breeder of registered Poland China Hogs.

When farmers gathered, they would often discuss their hog breed preferences with a lot of fervor. These discussions were not limited to hog varieties. Varietal choices also existed for breeding cattle, milk cows or horses. The farm wife also used her information and personal choices in selecting the breed of chickens she thought best. Some breeds were better egg producers, while others produced more meat per bird. Sometimes farmers would choose several varieties of seed for cropping. Sowing an early and later maturing variety of wheat allowed harvesting to be spread out over a longer time period so work demands could be more easily met.

Hogs are scavengers like chickens, and many farmers who fed cattle ran a few hogs with them to get what grain went through the cattle. Fattening hogs required a lot of grain. As mechanization arrived on the farm, the tractor, grain grinders, feed wagons, and self-feeders helped cut the labor demands of feeding hogs. Soon the slop barrel disappeared.

The problem with raising hogs was the wide fluctuation of prices. Since a brood sow could produce from six to ten pigs in a short gestation, the market could be flooded in a hurry. When the market was good, everyone bought several sows and started raising pigs. By the time they were ready for market, the price would often have fallen to break-even or lower.

Dad would listen to the morning radio and find out that hogs in Wichita were bringing two-and-a-half cents per pound. In a few minutes a truck would arrive to pick up his shipment of hogs. By noon, as the hogs were arriving at the market, the price might fall to two cents. "That's unfair," he would say. "My pigs' bacon tasted just as good when they got to Wichita as it did when they left here in the morning."

Once Dad uncovered a cache of bootleg liquor and, after filling the hog trough with slop, poured some of liquor into the trough. The pigs stopped feeding, looked up at him, and squealed their displeasure.

A neighbor, when told of this experiment, thought that it was a waste of "good stuff." This fellow drank too much of the jug Dad had given him, became noisy, and was shut in the barn by his wife and son when some neighbors came that evening to visit.

This wife had been an orphan girl when a woman owning a bar in Chicago took her to raise. Closing the bar in early mornings, the lady would give the moneybags to the girl while she carried a brace of pistols to help them get home. The girl had a pistol when she lived across from us. One night there was a commotion in her chicken house, a suggestion of thievery. Mrs. G. grabbed her pistol and ran out the door. The thief heard the screen door slam. Leaving the chicken house, he ran across a moonlit field and pasture. He had to keep running as the barefoot lady was after him, screaming seamy Chicago language in his direction. She probably fired a shot or two.

Chicken prices often fluctuated like hog prices, as it was easy to develop a flock and start selling fryers. Every farm maintained a small flock to provide eggs and chickens for the family to eat. Sometimes the farm family would choose to raise a crop of fryers. When these young chickens were ready to sell, a call was made to a buyer, who came to the farm to collect them.

Many farms had a brooder house specifically for starting and developing young chicks. It was kept warm by a brooder stove that burned kerosene and had a thermostat to regulate the temperature. Self-feeders and watering devices helped chicks get off to a good start.

Adolescent chicks were divided, with the cockerels being sold to a butcher, canned, or in later years after home freezers were sold, frozen for the farm family. Pullets were grown for egg production in the henhouse.

Seldom do we hear much about the noise on a farm, but the sound coming from a happy hen house was music to a farm wife's ears. The money made from selling eggs was often designated as her grocery money. It was also fun to watch and listen to the young cockerels practicing to become a rooster: trying their crowing and strutting routines.

In the middle of the twentieth century, a number of large fryer producers began operation. Large operators were able to produce fryers more cheaply than the family farms. These big producers also began to build egg production facilities for thousands of hens at one site, so production of home fryers and eggs all but ceased. Farmers then just kept a few chickens for eating and producing the eggs the family needed. Now, neither fryers nor eggs are present on most farms. The ebb and flow principle was at work again.

In those days, everyone had a few milk cows and a cream separator. Dad usually had a dozen milkers. Our herd was a nondescript group: a brindle, a Hereford, a Jersey, a Holstein, and several Heinz 57s. When an auctioneer was selling a Jersey, he said it was the breed to buy, as her milk was so rich a silver dollar couldn't be seen at the bottom of the quarter full bucket of milk. Then, he added, a Holstein's milk had so little fat that a silver dollar would be visible through a full bucket of milk. When selling a Holstein, the same auctioneer remarked it was the right breed, as a Jersey didn't give enough milk to cover a silver dollar on the bucket bottom.

In the summer Dad's milk cows were moved to pasture three-quarters of a mile east. This meant we had to drive the car over there for morning and evening milking, haul the milk home, and separate it. Since Dad was farming a lot of ground, he had to stay in the field as long as he could see. By the time he got to the pasture in the evening, he used the car headlights to round up the cows.

To hurry the process, the whole family helped with the milking. My sister Phyllis and I learned to ride in the back seat of the family car with our legs between the five-gallon milk cans. Milking in the dark was not too bad once you got in the proper position. Once the bucket was between the knees, the rest was simple. You didn't need lights to know when there was no more milk.

After the milk and cream were separated, the skim milk was carried to the hog house and dumped into the empty slop barrel. A five-gallon bucket of milk in each hand made a heavy load, especially when the person carrying them had worked in the field all day.

I remember with pleasure several trips I made carrying milk. My favorite ones were in winter with snow crunching under my overshoes and the honking of geese migrating overhead on a moonlit night, a delightful combination. I also found beauty in the whistle of a steam train, as it roared through the night several miles away.

Cream was sold as sour cream for several reasons. The farmers did not have refrigeration in those days, and they couldn't spare time or gasoline to haul the cream several miles to a cream station in town every day.

In the thirties, I remember, two or three cream-and-egg stations existed in each little town; Aulne had one such station in its better days. Each station posted its egg and cream prices on a window, similar to the way gas stations post their prices out front. We would drive by the stations to see which was paying the higher prices.

At the cream station, someone took a measured sample of the soured cream and placed it into a small, long-necked glass container. As the container was spun in the centrifuge, the heavier milk solids sank to the bottom of the container and the cream rose into the calibrated neck. Based on this test, the farmer's pay was calculated on the amount of butterfat-the only thing the station was purchasing. Another worker washed the emptied cream cans and put them on the curb for the farmer to collect on his way home.

These stations shipped cream on the daily trains that made milk stops; hence the name, "milk runs" or "milk trains." The cream went to large creameries in big cities. The Hillsboro Co-op Creamery started making daily pickups at farms around mid-century. As a result, cream was sweet rather than the traditional sour cream. Creameries were able to buy cream in both conditions. Cream stations began to disappear due to this competitor. They, like the hired hand, the passenger train, and stockyards were caught in an ebb tide.

There was a lot of work around the cream station on Saturday night in addition to cream testing. Cases of eggs were also left at the local cream station. The work centered on checking quantity and quality. "Don't forget to candle every egg," the owner would tell his son, who helped on Saturday nights. Candling meant holding the egg to an inch-wide hole in a box containing a light. Rotating the egg with his fingers, the boy would get an indication of its condition. If blood spots or other imperfections were noted, the egg would be discarded. Farmers were paid accordingly. With many cases of eggs arriving early in the evening, someone did a lot of candling.

With four or more farms on each section of land, a lot of eggs and cream were sold in town, particularly on Saturday night. The little cream stations would take their larger cans and cases to the depot for shipment to the large creameries and egg buyers in the cities.

Louis usually ran a herd of three dozen Hereford beef cows. Pasturing began the first of May when the bluestem grass had developed to provide adequate growth. It was always fun to drive the cattle the mile and a half to the summer pasture in Fairplay Township. This pasture was just across the road from the one our milk cows used in Catlin Township. The corral gate would be opened, and the cattle driven out onto the road, which was U. S. Highway 50. Old Mitch, a Hereford with a stub horn, would take the lead, while the rest tried to keep up with her. Our car went ahead of the cows to make sure that all the neighbors' field gates were closed. I followed the herd with the rubber-tired tractor shifted into the road-speed gear to keep up with them. The cows called the calves that had become separated from them on the drive. The gate to the large pasture was opened, the cattle driven through. Our local cattle drive was over. The family enjoyed the day as the drive meant no more hauling silage or hay to the corralled herd. Summer had arrived at last. The cattle would eat fresh grass, and the feeding chores would be over for the farmer until fall.

In the early part of the twentieth century nearly every farm had some type of livestock fattening operation. Cattle feeding chores were totally over by spring if the farmer was fattening cattle for the butcher trade. He needed his time for fieldwork. In those years, most farmers fed a few head of calves for market. Besides raising hogs, this was a good way to market the grain they had raised as well as surplus forage. Some farmers bought extra calves to make cattle feeding a sizable sideline. Like hog feeding, fattening cattle could be risky from a profit standpoint.

Fattening hogs might continue with the use of self-feeders to take less of the farmer's time. In Andy's time, before trucks, fattened cattle were herded to the Aulne stockyards and sent up the loading ramps to the train cattle cars. Fat pigs were often loaded into a wagon for the transport.

Like chickens, hogs and dairy cows began disappearing as the size of farm families became smaller and farmers started specializing.

With less hired help and less diversification, the fattening process began to shift from the family farm to the larger emerging specialty operators. Now only a few feed yards fatten most of the animals, whether they are cattle, hogs, turkeys, or chickens. Fattening livestock has become a corporate activity. One seldom sees livestock on the Midwest farmsteads today. Corral fences have been removed, and fields of crops extend to the now empty barns, if indeed the barn and outbuildings even remain. Diversification, which was once the

Don and his parents.

strength of small farms and their guarantee that some of the activities would see them through tough times, is gone. Expertise in specialization serves the same role today.

The big grain farmer uses the Board of Trade to hedge his cropping bets. The Board of Trade exists to buy and sell farm commodities on a futures market, much as the stock market serves to invest in the futures of corporations and their products. Another hedge against going broke may be the jobs in town for the farmer and his wife. In the last fifty years farming has become a night and weekend vocation for many farmers. Much of the rural romance has disappeared.

The winter corrals suffered from rain and snow. Muck in the corrals became deeper and harder to walk through. Andy dropped his grinning chin forward to the left as he remembered what one bad winter meant to his hired man Hans. "Hans vas 'elping drive de fat steers into de barn ven vone turned and started running back. Hans vaved and shouted but de steer kept cummin. Hans' rubber boots became stuck in de muck and 'ee couldn't move out of de vay. De steer flattened de pur guy as it ran ober 'im."

It was a banner day when Louis bought a silo. "Instead of putting forage bundles into shocks in the field to be hauled to the corral when needed, the cane bundles would be chopped and blown into the silo. I think the ol' cows will like a hot meal next winter," he reasoned. The fermentation of the sugar in the food in tight confinement produced heat, which cooked the forage and its grain. At that point, it became silage or sometimes called ensilage. It was more fun to load warm ensilage from the silo out of the wind than to load bundles in a field with the wind-driven snow chilling a farmer's body.

Andy was ready to stop farming. Would Louis take over the farm? And like his dad, would he pick the wrong woman?

Chapter 7

Grace and Louis
My Parents Had a Full Life

Louis went to the city for social whirls
And courted the town's pretty girls.
They said, "No, not on your life
I don't want to be a farmer's wife."

Andy and Nettie were packed and moved out.
Grace and Louis were wed and she moved in,
They were chivareed, oh what a din!
They were going to be happy without a doubt.

Louis's wife, Grace was a Winkley. Her dad, Henry, had farmed two miles west of Aulne before running a Ford garage in Marion. Like his dad, Louis chose a schoolmarm. After high school she earned her teaching certificate at Emporia State College before teaching in several one-room schools.

Mother's family lineage was interesting. In pioneer days, losing a mate was common. Medicine was not well developed and living conditions lacked many refinements. Many times people died not of the primary problem, but from later complications. Life spans were short, and often a parent would die before the children were grown. The surviving spouse would generally remarry to finish the child-rearing process.

Mother had two grandfathers who had children before losing their wives. Each married a widow who also had several children. Her grandpa Kannengiesser married his sister-in-law. The new family consisted of two sets of brothers and sisters who were also each other's cousins. For both men, their subsequent marriages brought several additional children who were half brothers and sisters to the older children. To confuse the issue further, some of the unrelated stepchildren of Grace's grandfather Winkley married each other.

We children and grandchildren had difficulty knowing why some people were relatives and how the relationships occurred. Did Grace have step-aunts and uncles or were they half aunts and uncles? A child learned to recognize some of its relatives at the annual Winkley reunion

Perhaps next year their relationships to other people would become clear. It took a number of years to understand the complex family tree structure. It was more of a family grove than a family tree.

My grandmother was Clara Mae Kannengiesser Winkley. Her maiden name, Kannengiesser, was as German as her husband's was English. When Clara and Henry fell on hard times late in life, she paid off the farm mortgage by baking cookies and cakes, which she sold on the steps of a Marion bank. Back when long distance calls were made only to report a death or a birth, she and her sisters and half sisters kept in touch with a Round Robin letter. Each of five ladies had a letter in an envelope. When it came to one, she tossed hers and read the other four's letters. The new one she wrote was inserted before forwarding the large envelope to the next lady.

Though Henry was known to be ornery, when Clara wasn't watching, he also enjoyed light humor and became the source of a lot of amusement to the family. The family would laugh not only with him, but also sometimes at him. One time at a Winkley reunion, when he was in his seventies, he decided to go down the very tall, slipper slide in the city park. Once he was at the top of it, with other men noticing him, there was nothing to do but slide down amid all the "Be careful, Henry!" calls from the women. He forgot to put his feet down and landed sitting on the ground amid laughter from the family audience.

One of his mistakes was remembered for years afterward. He used various potions to rub on his sensitive skin. One evening before bed, Clara heard, "Mom. Oh Mom! What is this stuff?" With his glasses off, Henry had found a small saucer of varnish she had used earlier, and was trying to rub in into his hair and scalp.

One favorite family anecdote concerns Henry and brother, Charles, living as bachelors in a barn before a house was built. It was dark when Henry went to lie down. A cat was on the bed, so he picked it up and hurled it toward the open barn window. Just then Charles walked undressed in front of the window heading toward his cot. Surprise! A flying cat with all claws unsheathed!

Henry was fascinated by life around him. In contrast, Andy was turned off by it. Henry read and followed the news religiously until he died.

Grace's younger and only sister, Alice, also became a teacher. After contracting TB, she moved to a sanatorium in the hills near Livermore, California. After being cured, she stayed on to teach at the facility. When the number of TB cases decreased, the place was closed. My aunt then moved to town, married, and taught in the city high school. One night her cat awakened the family and they found the house was afire. Quick action minimized the damage.

Alice and Grace had twin brothers, Earnest and Earl, who were the apples of Clara's eye. Even though they were full of their dad's orneriness, Clara allowed them to get away with it; however, Clara still kept Henry in tow. The boys played football in high school and college where they were known as Big Wink and Little Wink.

In midlife, Earnest had an abdominal operation and didn't recover very well. His doctor friend went in again for exploratory purposes and found a sponge he hadn't removed the first time. This discovery shook the doctor so badly that he then didn't remove enough of the newly infected intestine. Later Earnest had to be hauled across several counties to Wichita for emergency surgery. Was he happy to flush the toilet the first time after that! He yelled, "Nursie, Nursie, come look at what I did!" The whole hospital ward knew about it and shared his happiness.

Earl was a bachelor much of his life. He married late, and like both his grandpas lost his mate, but he finished raising his daughter alone. He spent the last part of his life somewhat crippled. He fell off his riding lawnmower, which came back to run over him when he couldn't move out of its path. He died shortly afterward from his wounds.

Grace moves in as Mrs. Larsen.

Louis met Grace in the Aulne social scene. Aulne, a town of several hundred, grew on both sides of the Rock Island Railroad line. In the horse-and-buggy era, farmers drove to the closest town for commerce and other needs. Similar to the other small farm towns, Aulne had a depot, stockyards, a grain elevator, a drygoods store, a butchershop, and a phone exchange. There was also a blacksmith shop, at least two groceries, a cream-and-egg station, and a large community hall.

There was also the Aulne State Bank, which unfortunately both Andy and Henry partially owned through purchases of its stock. Banker Johnson mixed bank money with the money he got from raising registered Poland China hogs. When the courts finished with him, he left the hog pen for the state penitentiary. Imagine a banker raising hogs after hours!

With a sizable rural and village population, Aulne had church and community activities as well as private parties. Grace and Louis met there. Romance followed and marriage also. Aulne's tide was rising. Would it continue or ebb?

Louis's parents, Andy and Nettie, thought the Winkleys were "uppity," a reaction that was perhaps similar to what Mrs. Lovesee had said about Andy in the letter to Mrs. Clausen.

Grace settled into the role of a farmer's wife, an extension of her life on a farm as a girl. She raised a large garden, canned more food than was needed, raised chickens, helped with the milking, baked all their bread, and supported the local church. She later joined a number of clubs and associations, such as the Farm Bureau, church groups, and a neighborhood club called The Helping Hand.

She was a good cook and baker. Her cakes, cookies, and homemade candy were well known, but her cinnamon rolls and pies earned her fame. Neighbor women who had trouble with pie crusts used to marvel at "how Grace's pie crusts always came out great!"

During the Depression of the 1930s, the home demonstration unit of the Farm Bureau taught rural women to make several varieties of cheese, and Mother practiced this task. After the milk and the added ingredients curdled, she strained the cheese through cheesecloth or an old, clean curtain. Then she placed the curds and cheesecloth in a sausage press and cranked the pressing plate downward to squeeze the rest of the whey from the curds. Something placed against the crank kept it in the squeeze position until the cheese wheel became firm.

Mother always canned beef and sausage. She fried the sausage as patties, placed them in a glass jars in both quart and half-gallon sizes, then covered them with melted lard. To make sausage links, casings were pushed onto a tin tube extending from the sausage press. With the press full of the ground meat, she turned the crank to extrude the sausage into the casing. The filled casings were twisted every few inches to form links. Links were fried and, like the patties, were put into jars and covered with lard.

She raised chickens and eggs to sell. We ate a lot of fried chicken. After the chickens became older, the preparation changed to boiled chicken and noodles, which were homemade and sliced very fine. When the local butcher installed a series of frozen food lockers, Mother and Dad, like many other farmers, stored chickens and a lot of beef there. After World War II, they bought a home freezer and the frozen chickens stayed on the back porch.

Mom never learned to like lamb, milk, or the brains she fried for Louis after butchering. Making lard, a smelly chore, gave her the shortening she needed for baking and cooking.

Her basement stayed filled to capacity with her canned meat, vegetables, and fruit. However, some jars of food would spoil. Often when she was gone and Dad happened to come to the house, he would remove an armload of jars from the basement to discard. Later she would scold, "Louis, you have been in the basement again. I don't like it, let me take care of that." He seldom got away with this kind of helping!

Mother had her pride. Whether that came from the German heritage of the Kannengiesser family or the English from the Winkley lineage, I never knew. In fact, I would guess she received an ample dosage from both lines. The pride did not run to vanity or outward dress. Rather, correctness of living and proper ways of doing things were important to her. She never entered a beauty shop, had nails done, or used cosmetics other than facial powder. Her hair was drawn back into a bun at the nape of the neck. She didn't purchase a lot of new clothes. This was the age of frugality and a lot of clothes were homemade. The treadle sewing machine became to the farm wife what the team of horses was to her mate. There was a Penney's store in each little town, and it was popular with both men and women when they needed clothing that couldn't be homemade.

Dad, like his sister Nancy, enjoyed children. He had a collection of simple toys that he kept for any kids who came with their parents to visit. He shared the toys with relish. He had puzzles made of wire and wood, and magnets with figures of children or dogs glued on top bent forward with lips puckered. The children couldn't resist when the magnets pulled the figures together. They were known as the kissers.

Dad also enjoyed peppermints, and usually had a sack of them in his pocket when he went out in later years. They were available for him to savor at church or to share with children. He was generous in other ways and enjoyed visiting older friends together with Grace.

Like his mother, Dad suffered from sleepiness. He could have a good night of sleep yet drop a forkful of food about to enter his mouth as he fell asleep at lunch. He was lucky to have only one accident due to sleepiness while driving. Creeping to a stop sign in Peabody, he dozed off and ran into a parked car. He did go to sleep on the tractor a number of times. If he was plowing, he would awaken as a tractor wheel left the furrow. However, this didn't happen if he was combining; in that case he would have to go back for the grain he bypassed.

Late in their life, when Dad had a brief stay in the hospital, Mother went looking for a house for sale in the town of Marion. A grandson, Larry, who is our oldest son, would take over the farm. Mother thought, "This will be great, for I'll be able to see neighbors and I'll be close to stores. Best of all, we won't be stuck in the country with bad roads if either one of us gets sick, which seems to happen more often than in years past." The garden was much smaller and she thought, "Louis can garden. It will give him something to do, and he needs to be outside; he can't just sit around. On nice Sundays we can drive to Aulne for church. After all, it's only eight miles."

She continued to count their blessings: "Although Don and Jacquie are in California and Phyllis and Owen live in western Kansas, we have grandchildren and great grandchildren nearby." Grace and Louis were lucky, she reasoned. The Louis Larsens began enjoying this life they had worked so hard to achieve. Sadly, Mother passed away after a few years of the so-called retirement.

Their moving to town followed a pattern: farmers had been moving to town for the past several decades. In earlier years aging parents had moved in with their children. Many homes housed parts of three generations. Children knew their grandparents quite well. But in mid-century many farmers decided, "I think we'll try to retire early and move to town!" This worked well for the wives, but many men found it hard to adjust to the change. A lot of men passed away after only a few years, resulting in small towns of farm widows, living alone.

Grace and Louis, celebrate fifty years..

Dad lived for a number of years after Mother's passing. He lived by himself a few years in the Marion house before moving to Peabody. There, he lived in an apartment owned by Larry, who had quit farming the family farm to help his wife, Sue, run a basket manufacturing company in Peabody.

This was fortunate, as Dad and Larry were special to each other. When Larry was a baby, if he cried my mother would take him from Jacquie or me to quiet him. He would continue to cry and reach for Dad. The minute he was in Louis's arms, Larry became quiet and snuggled to his grandpa. This was almost too much for Mother to take. Dad had all he could do to keep his feelings of pride and happiness from showing and making Mother feel even worse. This special relationship continued into Dad's final years.

Dad found a lot to keep himself occupied and he developed a routine for the day. On arising, he would eat breakfast and then go to the grandson's little basket store and factory to see if any of the workers needed anything from uptown or if there were letters to mail. He would retrieve the mail from the store's postal box. By the time he returned, Larry would have dialed the store's TV to an animal program. Dad would sit in an easy chair Larry had positioned for him and enjoy the program. It would soon be time to return to the apartment before going to the senior center for lunch. The afternoon would include taking a nap, checking to see if he could help at the store, and watching more TV animals. These two men enjoyed and cared for each other.

Andy and Louis both had a number of horses, beef cattle, milk cows, a dozen or so yearling calves to fatten, and a herd of hogs. Louis would add turkeys and sheep in a decade or two. Since the land Andy chose to farm did not have springs or a creek, how did these two farmers manage to provide enough water for their livestock?

Also, was the dog associated with farms a pedigree pet or a mongrel farm staff member?

Chapter 8

Windmills, Cats and Dogs

Little Things Count

Stop the fieldwork, fix the mill
So the livestock can drink their fill.
Come on wind, let 'er blow
This old pump's got to go.

Water for the livestock could be a problem in both summer and winter. The livestock drank from large open containers, six to twelve feet across. The common name for the device depended on which animals drank from it. It could be called a horse tank or a cattle trough. Being shorter, sheep and hogs used a lower container. Louis found an old institutional, white enameled sink, five feet long and used it as a sheep-watering tank when he went into sheep raising in the 1940s. I don't think he told Grandpa that the unit came from the now defunct "poor farm."

Each of Louis's four corrals had these water tanks freeze in the winter. Several times a day a fence post would be used to break the ice so animals could have a drink.

When the Rural Electrification Agency, nicknamed the REA, brought electricity to the county in the end of the 1930s, an electric pump provided the sheep with fresh water from one of our wells. Each morning, if ice had formed during the night, it was thrown from the small trough before the pump was activated. When warmer water fresh from the well hit the cold cast iron container water vapor would rise into the air, making the water appear to steam as if it were slowly boiling.

This well was in the middle of the farmyard and was known as a dug well, the same type as the well Andy and Clausen dug for the schoolhouse. Its wall was made of flat stones laid on each other in a diameter of three feet. It was about twenty-five feet deep. A second well on the other side of the barn had been drilled by a well-digging machine. This well's wall was a six-inch steel pipe called a well casing. The wells we used in the pastures were drilled wells.

All but one of the four wells had a windmill to operate a pump. (Americans know Kansas for its wind. Just think of Dorothy in *The Wizard of Oz*, or reading other tales of its tornadoes). The tower above the well on the backside of the barn did not have a windmill fan or mechanical head to pull the pump rod to raise water from the well.

During the Great Depression, Dad could not afford to buy what was needed, so he improvised. He fashioned two walking beams and attached one to the top of the each tower. He ran heavy wires from the ends of the first beam over the top of the barn roof ridge to the other beam. The job was finished with a clutch arrangement that allowed him to operate either pump from the one windmill.

One day the main well went dry. On raising the cover Louis found a snake at the bottom of the well, a common find in dug wells. Taking a bar, Dad descended, killed the snake, and began trying to break a large rock in the well bottom. Once he cracked the rock, water flowed into the well from the crack. The well never went dry again.

In the summer, at least two tanks were used for the pasture cattle in case the wind did not blow for several days. Louis was good at solving the problem of no wind for pumping. He used a small pipe bent into a U-shape as a siphon to transfer water into the second tank. When the wind resumed, he would have two full tanks. He maximized his chances of having enough water.

Dad showed a couple who were renting the house near one pasture how to start the siphon. He immersed the bent pipe into water, filled it up and closing both ends with fingers. He then turned it over and lowered each end into a different tank. Air pressure caused water to flow through the siphon, from the tank with the most water into the less full tank.

In a few days the lady asked, "Louis, show me how to start the siphon again. My husband told me I should suck on one end. I nearly drowned trying that method." Her husband, Alfred, was not one to show her how to do the sucking. He was better at telling how things should be done.

Alfred was a cousin of Dad's. Aunt Maggie, Grandpa's sister, was rocking Alfred as a baby one stormy day when a ball of lightning came down the fireplace and crossed over them. Alfred suffered from a shriveled arm after that experience.

In the Flint Hills area, a few miles east of the Larsen farm, a summer without much rain or wind could cause water problems for the ranchers, as creeks and wells could go dry. The ranchers would have to haul water from other areas or sell the cattle earlier than planned.

There is little sand in the substrata under Marion County for filtering purposes, thus underground water became polluted. Water via a pipeline from another part of the state now supplies drinking water to many farms.

The electric pump Dad installed in the farmyard well midcentury now gave the house running water. Up to that time, roof runoff was directed into a cistern, from which it was pumped for family drinking water.

One day, after noticing the water had begun to have an odor, Louis lifted the cover to investigate the condition of the cistern. He saw what was left of a missing cat. The remains were fifteen inches wide and three foot long. Needless to say, not only did the family pump the cistern dry; they cleaned and rinsed the sides and bottom of it. Unfortunately, the huge cistern had been nearly full.

For several years Dad enjoyed raising turkeys. The young toms would strut toward him. He would mock their odd strutting noise, "Stuuck," and move toward them with his arms hanging down and outward similar to their wings. This interaction with his animals was part of his joy of farming.

A grasshopper invasion occurred one year and suddenly he noticed his turkeys were missing. They had gone grasshopper hunting. Walking turkeys frightened the hoppers, causing them to hop or fly. The birds followed the hoppers until the flock was well away from our farm. We finally located them on the Townsend Ranch, a mile east and three miles south.

We had to walk them home taking care not to alarm them. If poults, young turkeys, became frightened they can trample each other to death. This can occur if they are in a pen and see a hawk or a low-flying airplane.

Catching mature turkeys for market can also be interesting. Claws catch on pockets and wing-bones bang on heads and elbows, inflicting bruises and tearing clothing.

The roles of farm cats and dogs should not be forgotten. The dog was a visible help. He served as the farm's local deputy, if not the sheriff. His duties included keeping away many bad guys and catching others: rats, opossums, and rabbits. Announcing visitors, whether humans or a bull on the loose, was also part of his job description. As the farmer loaded bundles from shocks in the field onto the hayrack, the dog was there to catch any mice, rats, or snakes that might be present. This four-legged partner helped round up any animals that found a way to escape their pens. It was always surprising to notice how, when pigs heard the loud call, "Here, Stub, here, Stub," they remembered where the hole was in the fence to get back into their pen. They escaped ear bites if they beat Stub to the fence.

Grandpa Andy and Stub. enjoying the winter sun.

The cats were mousers, and with all the grain and hiding places they earned their keep. A favorite with my sister, Phyllis, and me, was Tanzy, a three-colored cat. In genetics class I learned that sex linking determines that all three-color cats are females. When we collected wood from the woodpile for the stoves, Tanzy would meet us, crawl onto the shoulder of our mackinaw, and ride into the house. Mother couldn't touch cats for some deep-seated reason; however, Tanzy was welcome in the house, as she jumped into the kitchen woodbox and sometimes found a mouse, to Mother's delight. "You're a good cat!" Mom said from a distance.

Early in our marriage Jacquie and I had a nice black tomcat. We had two babies, and Tom played with them until he became mature and no longer came home at night. One day Dad and I were using a tool that puts rubber rings around lamb tails to dock the tails or around the scrotums of male lambs for castration purposes. This is the most painless of all methods, especially if it is done to the newly born animals before the blood and nerve circulation systems become well developed. In a few weeks tails and scrotums drop away. As we finished with the lambs, Tom came by. "Grab Tom!" Dad called. I did and Dad slipped a band on Tom's scrotum. Tom demonstrated no pain and didn't run away. He soon started staying in the house and let our children drag him around again.

The Hett boys, who lived two miles north of us "fixed" their toms a different way. On a rainy day when these seven brothers couldn't think of anything else to do, they would catch a tom for "fixin'." While one held a rubber boot as another boy or two would try to put the cat's head and front feet into the rubber boot, a very challenging task, as no cat wants to lose its feeling of being in charge! The tom would fight tooth and toenail, with a quickness second to no other animal. The boys had to be really committed to this challenge in order to try it. When the tom was in the boot with only his rear exposed, a snip with a sharp pocketknife and the tom was an ex-tom.

Farm cats would always show up at milking time. A stream of milk aimed at their faces would be welcomed as they lapped at it. They enjoyed a bit of warm milk. Tom liked this, also. Sometimes my orneriness showed as I let Tom have two streams aimed to his mouth. The fun began as I directed one stream toward one of Tom's ears. Tom responded by batting at one stream as if to bring it back into focus, his mouth. He would soon retire from the area and start his wash-up.

Rogue toms would show up from time to time, and they often killed kittens. One "yeller" tom was particularly bad. I prepared for him by running a wire from near the cat pan into the shop and tying it to a magneto. I fed the cats and sure enough Old Yeller also arrived. After looking around for dogs and naughty boys, he satisfied himself that the coast was clear. He happened to be sitting with his private parts on the wire when I gave the magneto a spin. Tom rose straight up three feet. The high voltage probably didn't hurt that part of him too badly. Yellow kittens were birthed for several more years.

It is no secret that oil lamps lit the houses of the past. Several farmers had gasoline lamps consisting of a mantle inside a glass chimney. These Aladdin lamps gave a very bright light, as the mantle glowed when it became quite hot. One could tell which families owned them by the brightness shining from a window as you drove past the farmhouse at night.

Dad installed a carbide gaslight system in the house early in his marriage. This system consisted of a large underground tank partly filled with water. Sacks of chemical dropped into the water generated the gas for lighting. The light produced was quite bright.

Any light needed in the hog house, the barn, or elsewhere outside was furnished by a kerosene lantern, which was carried about or hung from a nail. This was a lot cheaper than a flashlight as batteries did not last long at that time.

Sometime between the start of the Great Depression and the beginning of World War II, Dad bought an automatic Delco electric generator. As the old gas pipes were removed from the house, wires followed into the openings. When the 32-volt batteries ran low, the generator started itself and recharged them.

After several years, the REA, Rural Electrification Agency, appeared in the area. All that was required for us to go on line was to replace the lower volt light bulbs with 110-volt ones, and our electric lights continued.

With electricity, it was possible for a family to buy an electric refrigerator, if their crops were good enough to allow them to afford such a luxury. Up to that time, housewives had to store milk either in containers hanging on ropes in a dug well or in an icebox if they were fortunate enough to afford one.

One other option did exist, the gas-powered refrigerator. It worked similarly to the modern air conditioner: compressed gas was allowed to move through a small opening, causing cooling. Gas pressure was built by heating the refrigerant gas with a small fire in the refrigerator system. One such refrigerator was named

Electrolux Survel.

Before the REA, the only time most people used the icebox was in the summer during harvest. Going to town for ice was an expensive and time-consuming trip, so people avoided it. If someone was going to town, it was prudent to buy a block of ice for replacement purposes.

Dad would often buy the seventy-five-pound or one-hundred-pound block instead of a fifty-pound unit. He liked homemade ice cream and there was always plenty of milk and cream to make this treat. In fact, he saw ice cream more of a staple than a treat.

For a number of years, some farmers cooperatively cut ice in the winter from a pond a half mile south of Aulne. They stored the ice blocks in a hole in the ground, covering them with straw and dirt to insulate them from the spring and summer heat.

I've learned about the families and other help that worked the farms in the days following the breaking of the prairie into farmland. But what of the crops Andy grew? What did he do with his crops? As his son Louis took over the farm, did he change the tried and true methods of his dad? Did Andy ever own a tractor or a car?

Farming must be fun, because there are so many people doing it. Planting, cultivating and harvesting must be a kick, right?

Louis, Andy and Don.

Chapter 9

Fieldwork

Crops Replace the Bluestem

"Come on poise, get out ob bedt.
Bob, I vant you to take de two-row planter.
Louis, you are to use de two-row sled.
Cum on now, I vant you down 'ere on de canter.

Spring, with its changeable and fascinating weather, is a very important season on the farm. Sometimes fieldwork began even before spring arrived. If the wheat got a slow start in the previous fall, or if there was a lack of late fall rains, the wheat would not cover the ground completely. Over the winter, as moisture in the soil froze and thawed, clods and lumps would become quite fine and subject to blowing winds. With a strong and rising spring wind from the south, some soil particles would move across the soil surface and knock others into movement also. The field was then said to be "dusting" or "blowing," and it needed attention to keep the process from spreading. Cultivating implements were taken to the field to bring some moister soil and clods to the surface to stop the soil movement.

The worst dusting and dust storms occurred in the 1930s. I remember being in country school when the worst one of all happened. The sky began to darken and turn a greenish color. Miss Iva, the teacher of our one-room school, called lessons to a halt. She took the book she was reading to pupils and seated herself next to a window in order to have sufficient light for reading. After the blowing stopped, it was four o'clock and time to walk home. The children were fascinated with the dirt drifts across the ditches and roads.

The two neighbors to the south of the Larsen farm did not work their fields to stop the blowing. Their topsoil came through the hedgerows and made drifts fifteen to twenty feet out into our fields. Some of the drifts were two to three feet thick.

If the crops weren't planted between spring rains, there might be no harvest. Every minute counted. In the early part of the century, when farms were very diversified, there were also morning chores to be done before fieldwork could begin. It was important to start the day early to avoid wasting daylight.

Louis told of a neighbor who called his boy early in the morning in this manner: "Daavid, oh, Daavid, stand up, Daavid." As a boy, I could feel for Daavid. It seemed unreasonable to be in the field at seven after doing chores, eating breakfast and either putting gas in the tractor or harnessing the team. I never won the argument that it was too early!

The large tractor used in the 1940s had around twenty horsepower on the belt – perhaps ten when traveling and pulling an implement. When you compare that power with the power of a team of two or four horses, it is easy to understand why the average farm at the turn of the century was eighty acres and no larger. It took a lot of time for a horse farmer to prepare an acre for planting, to care for the growing crop, and to harvest it. Unlike a tractor, the team had only one working speed.

Most history books tell of John Deere inventing a new kind of plow, which made the breaking of the prairies possible. The tightly rooted sod of the prairie was too dense to be cut easily by the plows the first pioneers used in the eastern states prior to the mid 1800s. Challenged by this problem, Deere came up with a better design made of steel and began manufacturing his plows in the 1840s.

The lowest element of the plow, the share, has a forward nose that turns slightly downward to pull it into the ground. Levers on early plows and hydraulic cylinders on the current ones regulate the depth at which the share operates. The share is attached to the plow to be pulled through the ground at an angle for easier cutting of soil and roots. While the share may be up to eighteen inches long, it cuts a furrow that is only twelve or fourteen inches wide. Above the share is the moldboard, a polished and curved steel plate that lifts and turns the soil, causing it to fall upside down. Prairie plowing requires a lot of energy. When Andy broke prairie he had to use a plow that cut a single furrow to enable his team of two horses to be able to pull it. Later, a few early farmers had huge steam engines that could pull plows with several moleboards. These huge machines lasted only several decades. Soon with a small gasoline tractor, a farmer would refer to his plow as two twelves or two fourteens, the number and width of the furrows it created. Andy had finished farming when the small farm tractors made their appearance.

I couldn't crank it!

In the early 1930s, Dad started with a McCormick-Deering steel-wheeled tractor called the 10-20 that could pull a two-bottom plow. Andy shook his head in disgust seeing Dad's tractor. "Wit de 'orses, an old mare cun lay down and produce a foal to replace 'er. Dat tractor can't do dat!" Dad continued to use the 10-20 and later bought an additional three-wheeled type tractor with rubber tires.

In less than a century four different energy tides flowed into the prairie and three had ebbed completely. The oxen that pulled settlers' wagons into the prairies were quickly replaced by horses. The horse had a short time challenge from the large steam engines. A tide of plow type tractors on steel wheels began to share farm power requirements. A team of horses was able to out turn and maneuver the less maneuverable four wheel machine. The situation would change mid-century when McCormic Deering began producing a three-wheeled tractor branded the Farmall. This tractor could pivot on one wheel and was quite agile. While the older type tractor ebbed from the farm the Farmall configuration flowed into use at an accelerated pace when rubber tires replaced steel wheels and faster speeds were provided. Such is the ebb and flow or change. In a few years, four-wheel, rubber tired tractors would return in even larger sizes.

Once the turned soil had mellowed in the sun, rain, and perhaps some freezing, it was harrowed to break it into even finer particles and to fill any voids. When the soil was in proper condition and the season right, the crops were planted with a drill, a planter, or a lister.

The row crops as corn, sorghum, cane or soybeans were planted in furrows and cultivated several times to kill the crops of weeds that were sure to grow. Cultivating with horses meant that only one or two rows could be cultivated at a pass. I remember riding the cultivator the last time of the season. The corn was as high as my head as I sat low enough between the wheels to use the foot stirrups to guide the shovels toward or away from the plants. Since I couldn't see above the corn, the only view I had was the west-end of the mules headed east.

The crops were also harvested by horse-drawn equipment in the early years. When I was ten I had driven mules, and then Dad had me drive the 10-20 to pull a used combine he bought to harvest wheat. This harvesting machine could harvest a ten-foot wide swath at a time, needed an operator to ride it and adjust it. Later both he and I would pull smaller one-person combines we could adjust from the tractor seat. These were small units and advertised as "a family farm harvesting machine."

The self-propelled combine was the ultimate harvester, but due to the high price, the farmer needed a large acreage to make ownership practical. Again, the small farmer was being "squeezed out," as he couldn't easily compete. The small farmer's tide was ebbing.

Before the combine came into use, harvesting was an activity involving many processes: cutting, binding, shocking, and threshing. The first reaping machine took the place of the man with the scythe. As a team of horses pulled the reaper, it cut the grain stalks and moved them to the carrier part of the machine where they were held until a man walking beside the reaper pulled the accumulation onto the ground in a heap. In a few years the reaper became a binder as well, as the newer machines used twine to form and tie bundles of grain. These bundles were set up into shocks with the grain heads looking upward to await the threshing crew.

Neighbors formed a cooperative team called a threshing ring to provide for reciprocal help to thresh their grain. Now the threshing crews are a distant memory, because the combine does everything in one pass. Our first combine cut a swath of ten feet instead of the six-foot swath the earlier horse binder cut. It also moved at a faster pace.

Time is slashed when a truck takes grain from the combine on the move and speeds to sell it in a nearby town. In the older system the binder would have only cut the grain. There would be a lot of work to be done before the grain appeared in a horse-drawn grain wagon.

A romance accompanied a threshing crew even though threshing was associated with hard work and dirt. You learned to know your neighbors by working with them. I was twelve when I began running a bundle rack. First, I became adept at using a three-tined bundle fork to toss the bundles into the closed part of the rack. After the container part of the rack was full, the bundles had to land overlapping and sloping inward to build a self-supporting outer wall. When the four-sided wall was completed, more bundles were tossed inside. A properly laid load did not shift or slide off the rack as one traveled from the field to the farmstead where the threshing machine waited.

Andy's brother-in-law, Clyde, owned a threshing machine and

enjoyed operating and greasing it. That beat running a bundle rack and working up a sweat.

One neighbor thought Clyde should keep the grain placed properly in the grain wagon as other threshing machine owners did. This neighbor waited until Clyde was watching him and then climbed onto the grain wagon by grasping its sides in the middle and pulling himself up onto it. This bowed the side so the wagon could hold more grain. He then went to the other side and repeated the process. Clyde got paid for his threshing services by the bushel as measured by full fifty-bushel wagonloads. He saw he was being cheated by this neighbor's actions. In the future Clyde took care of the grain wagon.

Clyde's machine was small, requiring only one man to pitch bundles into it. Larger machines had more capacity and could handle the unloading or two bundle racks simultaneously, one on each side of the intake feeder. Of course, such machines took a larger threshing ring.

One new immigrant was assigned the job of spike pitcher. As he had no bundle rack or team, his job was to help others load their wagons in the field. At noon the theashing process stopped and the horses were watered as the last of the bundle racks came in from the field. The crew sometimes started eating before the last rack arrived with the spike pitcher.

One noon, the table was piled full of food, leaving no room for the bowl of gravy, so it was set on the plate in front of the chair, left for the spike pitcher. This poor fellow washed and sat down. Not knowing better, he assumed the bowl of gravy was the portion of food he was entitled to as spike pitcher, so he ate nothing but the gravy. The rest of the fellows watched and did not tell him otherwise. He missed out on the fried chicken, mashed potatoes, and corn on the cob.

The owner's wife served lunch midmorning and midafternoon both at the machine and from her car in the field. The menu: iced tea, Kool-Aid, and sandwiches.

A threshing machine directed the grainless straws into a large pile called a straw stack. When placed in a corral, the stack acted as food, bedding, and a winter windbreak for the livestock. Often small nocturnal animals burrowed into the stack for winter shelter. My sister, Phyllis, and I enjoyed climbing to the top of a stack to slide down the slippery slopes. Dad didn't approve of this, as footprints allowed rain and snow to enter the stack to start the spoiling process.

The farmer who had the threshers at his place kept busy pulling loaded wagons to the granary and scooping the grain into bins. Shoveling wheat wasn't bad, but the lighter-weight oats created a dust that caused one to itch in a few minutes. With sweat, this dust soon irritated considerably.

One time Dad pulled a four-wheel trailer to the granary and was confronted by his white tomcat asleep between the car tracks. It is said that most white cats are deaf and this tom did not hear the approaching car. It was impossible to stop the car with the heavy load pushing from behind. Dad straddled the cat while it slept on, not knowing how close to death he had been.

A bad storm could cause the dead stems of uncut wheat with heavy heads of grain to break and fall to the ground, making harvest impossible or the yield skimpy at best. During harvest, farmers with combines had to wait until any morning dew evaporated so the grain could be knocked from the heads. Once the heads of grain could be thrashed, the farmer would often continue after dark until the humidity rose enough to prevent efficient grain removal. Farm machines with headlights or operating lights became available at mid-century. That was an important advance. A new tidal advantage was flowing into the farmers tool kit.

Rains at harvest time helped weeds grow between the now dead grain stalks. These green, wet weeds made harvesting difficult. Bindweed, similar to a morning glory, arrived in this country as a hitchhiker. Its seeds were in the billeting straw of the ships carrying the Hessians who the British brought from Germany to fight for them in the war of 1812. When this weed binds the wheat stalks together into networks, serious problems develop. The combine chokes and stops. The operator has to remove panels and use a knife to cut and remove the tightly jammed, green blockage.

The grain plants shade the ground from any breezes or sunlight that could dry the soil. After rains, wet spots in the dirt can form and not dry, as the ripe wheat is dead and no longer uses moisture from the soil. The farmer will harvest around such wet areas, leaving them till last and hoping they will dry. If they are still wet when he tries to harvest them, he will unload the combine's grain bin to reduce the machine's weight. Hopefully, the lighter machine won't sink into the mud and become stuck.

With the arrival of the large self-propelled combines, the tides of binding, shocking, and threshing rings ebbed and they were not seen again.

Since wheat was harvested in summer, farmers often grew another grain crop needing a fall harvest, to spread their work and risk factors. Kaffir corn was a three-foot-tall row crop that was cultivated in early years by a horse-drawn sled and later with a sled mounted on a row-crop tractor. This too was a labor intensive crop. The next weeding was done with a cultivator until the rows of plants were tall enough to shade the ground and prevent weed growth. Stalks were cut with a corn binder and tied into bundles. These bundles were shocked before the heads of grain were separated from the stalks with a knife much the same as a papercutter knife

Milo-maise, nicknamed milo, is a short plant with its grain growing on a vertical head, similar to the kaffir corn it replaced. It was a better animal feed. When this grain was introduced, the small combine had just appeared and milo was harvested in the field. No wonder hired hands were no longer needed: downsizing, a word to be coined a half-century later, had begun in earnest. The word is a related synonym for ebbing.

Cane was also raised for cattle feed, as there was more sugar in the cane leaves and stalks than in the kaffir or milo. The five or six foot tall cane provided a lot of tonnage of feed per acre. When bundles of cane were shocked and later fed to cattle, dry stalks weren't too palatable. With the advent of the silo, it became easier to store the winter livestock feed. The amount and quality of the cane as livestock feed was improved. To make silage the cane stalks were cut by the ensilage cutter and blown into the airtight silo where the moisture and sugar in the cane heated and fermented. The silage provided a warm breakfast for the cattle.

Filling a silo by hand was hard work, as bundles six feet long needed to be loaded onto racks and taken to the ensilage cutter at the silo. Farmers soon learned how to lever long bundles with a swing to fling the bundle over their head and control its placement as the upper end of the bundle slipped through the farmer's gloved hand. An ensilage cutter at the base of the silo had its blower pipe rising to empty over the silo top. Bundles were fed into the cutter and blower combination. Shocking cane bundles and hauling them to the livestock in winter would ebb as fast as a farmer became converted to the new processes.

It seemed to farmers that just as they had installed and almost paid for a system to do the work, the equipment manufacturers came on the market with another system that was more efficient, saved more labor, and did the work faster. The new field cutters, pulled by a tractor, cut the forage in the field and blew it into a following wagon or trailer. No handwork was needed. Again the tide was changing. When the chopped forage filled the wagon pulled behind the cutter was full, it was taken to a blower at the silo.

Similarly, a simple machine was replacing the silo-filling ring. The farmer and his son could fill the silo themselves. This trailer not only caught the cut fodder; its movable floor carried the material into a blower at the base of the silo. It took a special skill to back a four-wheel trailer of ensilage to the blower-unloading zone. It was unnoticed by some, but the hired-man tide was completely out.

A few farms raised millet, flax, barley, soybeans, sown cane, and later, sunflowers. When the large heads of the sunflower hit the combine's beater, there was a loud noise like ongoing thunder.

Years ago corn was shucked by hand, one ear at a time. When shucking corn, a farmer would nail together a panel of boards, three feet tall, that attached to the side of a grain wagon commonly called a lumber wagon. This became known as the bang board.

The horse team started down the cornrows pulling the wagon.

The shucker placed a shucking or husking peg on his glove, ready to start the bangboard music. A husking peg or pin consisted of a metal hook riveted to a piece of leather with a pair of bands that hooked together on the back of the wearer' gloved hand and also on the fingers ahead of the knuckles. The metal curved upward and backward. The Husker would grab the ear of corn with his second hand and rake with the peg to jerk the husks open. He would jerk and twist the ear from the husks and stalk, and then throw it in the direction of the bangboard.

With practice, huskers did not look at the wagon, as they knew where the bangboard was. The bang of the ear indicated a hit, and by that time another ear was in the air. When the shucker reached the front of the wagon, he called for the horses to "get up," and then "whoa!" On reaching the end of the row, the horses were turned into the next group of rows, the bangboard changed to the other side of the wagon, and the process was repeated. In the early days this activity kept many boys out of school in early days until the corn harvest was completed.

When the wagon was full, the corn was taken to the farmstead and put into corncribs, buildings with sides of wire or slats that allowed air to reach the corn for further drying. These buildings are no longer present on farms. The word corn crib has probably ebbed from most vocabularies.

As the twentieth century ended, a tide of self-propelled corn huskers entered the cornfields. They would straddle four rows and move faster than the fellow with the peg on his glove could walk.

After the fall harvest, if the weather was favorable, cattle were turned into the milo, kaffir or cornfields to garner what roughage and dropped grain they could find. Corn was grown for its grain when farmers raised a lot of hogs or were fattening cattle.

Today, corn is a cash crop, as there are seldom any animals on most farms to fatten. The grain goes to the large feedlots and to food manufacturers. Machines harvest corn in today's cornfields, negating the need for shucking pins, bangboards or corncribs.

With mechanization, the need for horses and hired men faded and disappeared. While the size of farms increased and families became smaller, technology enabled the farmer and his son to manage on their own. Rubber tractor tires soon replaced steel lugs, and tractor lights became standard equipment.

All farm equipment manufacturers joined the movement to modernize farm machinery, making it adaptable or specialized, increasing its power and volume. These factories helped transform farming from a way for a farmer to make a living into making it a rural business enterprise. This was a major change in the tidal tables.

The family unit could farm more acreage. By the 1940s, the number of farms and farm families began to decrease. Unused farmhouses were being trucked down Highway 50 to Wichita to house defense workers in the aircraft industry during World War II.

A 1921 map shows that section 13 where Andy started farming and the eight sections touching it had forty-one farmsteads. In 1997 only eight farmsteads existed and couples inhabited but half of those. Many of the original eighty-acre farms supported families of five to eight. When I quit farming in the fifties, Dad and I were handling 720 acres. The rural population of Marion County grew from 700 in the eighteen-seventies to 22,000 in the 1880 census. In 1997 the population without counting the several small towns, had dropped to 8,400.

We have seen many tides rise and fall with many cresting in midcentury. Others might get their swells later. Would the tide tables change much in the future? Had the changes reached their end? Close the patent office, someone said, everything has been invented. Can there be more changes?

Dad will open a maternity ward in the barn. How could his cats and dog assist him in getting better results?

Chapter 10

Louis' New Love, Sheep

"Vy do you Vant Sheep?"

Dad certainly wasn't Little Bo Peep
But he definitely wanted some sheep.
In spite of noise, wool and smell
They all got along quite well.

Sheep were seldom seen in Marion County in the first half of the twentieth century. The flocks in the county numbered a dozen or fewer. Anyone who raised sheep was not considered much of a farmer, let alone a livestock person. Hogs and cattle were the livestock of the county, along with flocks of chickens.

As a boy, Louis learned to raise hogs and cattle by watching his dad. The farmstead was prepared for livestock production with barn, corrals, hog houses, and granaries. When Andy retired to live in an unoccupied farmstead, Father took over the farm and continued the cattle and hog tradition.

One day in the forties, Dad came home from the Dansken family farm sale just east of Aulne and announced he had purchased their flock of sheep. Andy had a fit! "You don't noo enyt'ing bout dem. Bedder stick vit vhat you noo bout: cattle und oogs." He carried on for several weeks.

Dad just laughed and said, "I think I'm smart enough to learn about sheep and their care." And to himself he probably thought, "When you started you only knew about geese and milling, not anything about cattle and hogs."

Andy just shook his head, squinted with a hard face, and walked away. He had heard how nobody liked mutton. It "schmelled!" Was this true, or was it a rumor fostered by the beef producers? The family learned to cook lamb and like it. No one remembers Andy turning down any lamb later whenever it was served him. If lamb "schmelled," it schmelled better than the barrel of sauerkraut.

When Andy was farming the land, he had the home quarter section fenced with hog wire, which later helped keep sheep from escaping for the most part. However, Dad ordered a trailerload of sheep wire from Montgomery Ward to be delivered by rail to Peabody and he soon had a proper sheep fence. Over the years the flock grew until it numbered 250 ewes and three or four rams. The trailer was pulled to town for more fencing material.

When one ewe found a hole in a fence, the rest of the flock quickly learned about it and immediately followed her out. Dad would say, "I think they have a special bleat that means, 'Here's a hole. Come on, let's get out and go!'" The idea was to stop the first one.

Mother was concerned that the best fence should be around her house yard, which contained her garden and flowers. After a winter in the corral, the ewes thought Mother's flowers would be like dessert. She did not like to touch the sheep, but if someone left a gate open she became a real zealot in herding them out of her flowerbed. Those occasions were as close as she ever came to uttering naughty words.

The County Farm Bureau agent drummed up interest in starting small flocks. He stated that the sale of the fleece paid for the ewe's keep while the lamb was profit. This proved to be true in most cases. With orders in their pockets, County Agent Hagins and Bill Amick, an experienced sheep man, caught a train to the Southwest and bought yearling ewes called Western ewes. Western was the term applied to all range sheep from the Southwest. When the ewes arrived by the Rock Island Railroad in Aulne, the would-be shepherds arrived with all sorts of conveyances to take their starter flocks home. Now all the new shepherds needed was a ram, or as we called them, a buck. The agent went to a ranch elsewhere and bought rams for those farmers starting flocks.

Over the years the number of ewe imports increased, and soon Aulne shipped more spring lambs to market than anywhere else in the state. When farm work was "laidby" in the fall, a shepherd's dinner was held, with lamb as the main dish, and the little industry was praised and toasted. The featured speaker would be from the Animal Husbandry Department at Kansas State College.

Here is where the sheepmen heard a lot of interesting stories, such as how the Navajo counted sheep. They took up a handful of pebbles and every time ten sheep ran past them, they dropped a pebble. When the last sheep was gone, they counted the pebbles, multiplied the number of pebbles dropped by ten, and added the number of single sheep counted since the last dropped pebble. In this way they arrived at the total count. It was never explained how the counter was able to count the sheep as they ran by him, usually at top speed with a third of them jumping high into the air.

It was rather dangerous to introduce a new ram into a flock, as there was a lot of heavy fighting among the rams to determine the pecking order. Two rams would back off, then rush full speed to hit each other in the head. One way to let them get acquainted was to put all of the rams together in one very small pen for several days. They were not able to back away very far, so they spent the days swinging heads or charging each other across only the two or three feet of space available to them. No one got hurt and the social order was eventually established. Someone would capitulate and the issue would be resolved.

One neighbor put his new ram into a pen beside the resident rams' pen. The newcomer and another ram met at the fence and then backed off, step by step for quite a distance before charging at top speed towards each other. Next morning the new, several-hundred-dollar ram was lying dead beside the fence. They had met at the fence with such force that the newcomer's neck was broken!

Young lambs also practiced head banging. Their playful bumping was more for jest and accuracy than for power and damage.

A new shepherd and his family also needed to remember the territorial interests of the ram. Territory was usually any place where the ram or his ewes were located. Oliver Tharp, a neighbor, used to tell of seeing his son, Max, come out of the grain shed one day with two buckets of grain. Oliver was not the only one who saw Max. His ram hit the boy from behind at full speed. Max and the two buckets flew through the air in three directions.

Our first ram connected with Dad the same way soon after becoming part of our flock. Dad then began to turn the ram's charge into a game. He placed his hands together, forward and to one side. This was the closest target so the ram hit his hands.

My father enjoyed this, and the ram was doing his duty of protecting his territory. But without any solid hits the ram soon tired of the game. Then Dad changed the game without telling the ram. He thought if the ram wanted a solid target, one could be provided. Dad stood still in front of a post until the ram was all but there and had closed its eyes prior to contact. Dad stepped aside. After a few head-ons with a big solid corral post, the ram learned not to charge if his owner was near a fence. One can quickly guess why the ram soon learned not to charge Louis if he was next to the barn. Another variation of the game involved an old tire tossed into the air as the charge developed. The ram, with a good aim, hit the center, ending up with a tire around his neck and a countenance of embarrassment on his face.

Dad would fool a charging ram by jumping up at the last minute, then coming down on the ram's back as he stopped where his tormentor had stood. Again, the ram always appeared embarrassed as he opened his eyes to view the situation.

When Mother caught Dad doing this, she would tell him, "Stop teasing the ram." She sided with the ram. "It isn't funny!"

He would reply, "Why, he is getting the satisfaction of being a good protector."

The barn had been built large for horses, so now, without them, there was a lot of room for the sheep. Letting them out of the barn in the morning could be dangerous, as they all wanted out first. When the door was opened slightly, the sheep would rush to exit. The flighty Western ewes would jump and often bang into the shepherd's body, try to run between his legs, or attempt to jump over him, usually all at the same time.

The correct procedure was to crack the door free of any frost, and then pull the door open on the run, so all the ewes could exit simultaneously. This procedure prevented a lot of injuries to pregnant ewes and small lambs. Once out, the sheep rushed to get a drink, ran to the feeders, or started a nervous and noisy search for the lamb that became separated from the mothers during the exit.

When the first lambs were a few days old, Dad would fix them a pen in a corner of the barn. He spaced slats far enough apart so the lambs could come and go but the ewes couldn't enter. One elderly ewe named Grandma always wanted to get to the special lamb feed (nice alfalfa hay and grain) that awaited the lambs in a feeder. It didn't take long for the lambs to accept this hospitality. The fattening process had started. As the lambs began to reach a hundred pounds, Dad began to think about the market.

After the lambing season was over, the rams were segregated and spent the spring and early summer as bachelors. In the late summer Louis let them in with the ewes so the lamb crop would arrive before the cold of winter. The early lambs were able to take the winter better than those born later. They would also be ready for market before fieldwork competed for our time. Prices were higher for the early spring lambs also.

One could usually predict that lambing would start with the first really cold snap when the thermometer would plunge to its very coldest range.

For our first morning activity in lambing season, Dad or I entered the barn to check for any new lambs. Usually Dad separated a ewe and her new lamb from the flock for a day or two. A heartbreak was to find a new lamb and no new mama. Then there was some detective work to find which ewe had just given birth.

In fairly nice weather before lambing started, the flock could be left to sleep in the corral. On several mornings we found a new lamb in the corral that had not risen on its feet quickly enough to nurse. It might be too chilled to survive without help. We took such lambs to the nursing station, which was usually in front of the open door of the kitchen stove. Once they had a sip of their mother's colostrum-laden first milk with its antibodies, they generally survived.

When the season was producing a lot of lambs, it was common to have several newborn animals in the kitchen getting dry and warm. It was heartening to bring in an almost lifeless lamb and later to return it to its mother. Sometimes a ewe would not accept her firstborn lamb, and usually there was a bottle lamb or two around the yard. Taking care of the bottle lambs was a chore for my sister Phyllis and me.

Dad enjoyed his sheep and tried very hard to keep from having bottle lambs, so he started an adoption agency. When a ewe lost a lamb at birth, he would find an orphan for her to adopt. This was contrary to the ewe's point of view: it wasn't her lamb, and she would butt it against a pen wall. To change the ewe's mind, Dad rubbed the orphan against the rear of the ewe, wetting the lamb with her spilled birth fluids. He also rubbed the dead lamb all over the orphan. This bothered the ewe, but she didn't fall for Dad's trickery. She continued to butt the little one.

Dad sometimes skinned the dead lamb and stitched the pelt together onto an orphan. Again the lamb was generally butted against the stall wall. In one case the process worked, and the shepherd forgot what he'd done until the lamb's overcoat began to rot and smell. He had to catch the adoptee and cut the lacings.

Probably the easiest ploy, and the one he enjoyed the most, was to place the ewe and orphan in close quarters in a penned-off section of the barn walkway and then feed the cats just outside the closed lower half of the door. The call, "Here, Kitty, Kitty, Kitty...." brought cats from various buildings to feed. The ewe's butting of the lamb was interrupted as cats were dropped one by one over the door into her stall.

The ewe's maternal instinct reacted, and any cat worth its salt was up and over the wall before it suffered a share of the ewe's butting and foot stomping. Then another cat would arrive in the pen, until Dad ran out of cats. After that treatment, the smart cats didn't come back to the breakfast pan for seconds that morning.

Old Stub, our dog, was always interested in the "Kitty, Kitty" call, and if he showed up, he went over the wall, also. Stub soon learned to climb the wall vertically like a cat rather than use the run-before-you-jump method of most dogs.

Sometimes this cat tactic for trying to stir the ewe's maternal urges worked. The family was never sure how much Dad's intention this procedure was to change the mind of the ewe and how much it was to have some fun at the cats' expense.

And then came Robbie. This orphan lamb was named not for a person but for the method he developed to feed himself. Father taught him to get warm milk directly from the source. Originally a healthy bottle lamb, Robbie learned to steal a snack as a ewe was caught by Dad and held for him. As soon as Robbie made contact with the serving table, the ewe began a rather vigorous hop-and-dance routine. What she lacked in choreography, she made up for with vigor and energy. Robbie learned to follow her lead in the dance, moving like a hummingbird feeding from a wind-blown flower. When Louis entered the sheepfold, Robbie would see him and follow like a pup, to be available should a ewe be caught.

Silage and grain were placed in long feeders before the ewes were allowed in this sheepfold where breakfast had just been served. Running to the feeders, the ewes pushed and crowded for a place. Once the feeders were crowded with ewes, Robbie would be turned loose to strike out on his own. Robbie couldn't take the normal side approach to the serving bar, as the adults were jammed tight against each other. So he made a rear approach. You guessed it, the ewe he chose, being wedged tight between other ewes, couldn't retreat to deal with him, so her rear began jumping and wiggling without Robbie missing a pull.

Then came the usual procedure when a ewe becomes nervous. She urinates. Poor Robbie had the dirtiest, smelliest, and brownest neck in the county. It's a wonder he didn't freeze his neck that winter. He was a true entrepreneur. Eventually, he didn't need to be fed with a bottle or to have one of us catch a ewe for him. Even when he was not visible to the eye, his presence was made known as a ewe's rear bobbed up and down somewhere around the feed trough. Robbie was not particular at this buffet table, and he served himself until he had his fill.

Robbie never had breakfast at Grandma Sheep's expense. She was never around the feed trough. This ewe aged prematurely and had a faraway look in her eye. Dad had nicknames for some of his animals and thought the name Grandma fit her quite well. She once got out and found that there was grain in the granary. Her life's goal was to get back into that building. As a result, she never ran to the sheep feeder in the lower corral with the others at feeding time. She had a number of contingency plans in case there was an opportunity to be seized. She would carefully position herself near the gate so she could make a pass to escape when the trailer of ensilage came into the pen. It took two persons to enter with the trailer: one to drive the tractor and the other to watch the gate and divert Grandma. She never learned, though what she lacked in success, she made up for in persistence. While the others ate, she checked and double-checked for any doors or gates left open. Daily, she would go to the lambs' area to see if she could squeeze through the special openings and investigate whether their trough had any overlooked grain. She never had a good pelt or a very good lamb. She was always waiting for her ship to arrive.

Raising sheep and running an adoption agency were not hard to learn, but could we learn to shear sheep? Who would teach us?

Chapter 11

Shearing and Shipping

A Different Spring Smell

It is a warm day in the spring
When you get the sacks and paper string
As the man takes out his shears
It's time for sheep to show their fears.

Shearing was a noisy and interesting time for the farm family, especially the kids and the dogs. The sheep would probably have used other descriptive words.

A good farm dog thought he was second in command of the activities and took an active interest in anything unusual or noisy. Our dog, Stub, a medium-sized terrier, colored orange and white, was raised from a pup. We got him from an elderly neighbor, "Pap" Hall, who bungled the tail-shortening process. He was supposed to have a short stub as many dogs do. Instead of an inch or two of tail, this pup was to carry a four-inch unit, hence the name Stub. He became a likable grown dog, devoted to the family and good at the usual dog chores: catching varmints, sounding alarms and being a good companion.

On shearing day he would announce a stranger's arrival and show continued interest as the visitor took tools from the car and started towards the barn. The sheep shearer had arrived. Stub also noticed the sheep were quite concerned about what was happening. What was bothering them? Could it be the strange odor coming from the man and his truck? Instead of going to lie under a favorite shade tree, Stub found a spot where he could keep an eye on the noisy sheep pen and shearing area.

Stub was correct about the odor: it was excess pelt grease from the man's past several week's work. It was strong and distinctive. One shearer slept in his car and also stored dirty clothes and tools there. The high-octane smell of this car could never be matched!

Shearing was scheduled late enough in the spring to allow the "yolk," or grease, to come out into the pelt. The yolk made shearing easier and the pelt weigh more. The added weight was important, as the wool was sold by the pound. Some people think the grease of the wool is lanolin, but lanolin comes from a gland just above the hooves. It is probably there to keep the hoof in good condition. It is certainly deodorized before it enters the cosmetic trade. If it weren't, no store would allow it on their premises. It would be the sauerkraut of any beauty shop.

The shearer used hand shears in the early days before the machine variety was developed. Shearing was backbreaking work, as one had to stand bent over all day. A good shearer would be able to work a hundred head of sheep in a day.

Once a ewe was caught, she was set on her rump, and would become rather docile. When the shearing was done and she was turned loose, it was interesting to watch her lamb and her friends get reacquainted with her. She looked very different wearing just her white underwear rather than the gray wool coat she left behind with the shearer.

Once removed, the fleece was rolled into a ball with the ends and odd pieces tucked into the center, and then tied with paper twine. There are stories of dead lambs, worn machine parts, rocks, and other items being rolled into the fleeces for cheating purposes, since the extra weight would bring the farmer more money. How much of this was true and how much was the itinerant shearer's story to impress a farm boy is hard to tell. Sheep shearers knew how to embroider a story for the local children's benefit.

A large jute bag, eight feet long and perhaps three feet across, was hung over a frame to receive the tied fleeces as they were thrown into it. Once a few fleeces were in the bag, my job was to get into the bag to tamp the fleeces tight so Dad didn't have to buy too many sacks. Once in the bag, I had to stay there without any fresh air until the bag was full; then I could climb out. After a few minutes in the bag with the smelly fleeces falling on my head, I began to smell like the shearer's car.

To schedule the shipping of the fat spring lambs, the County Agent worked with the Rock Island Railroad and a packing house in Kansas City. Several double-decker sheep cars were sent to wait on a siding in Aulne to transport the lambs. Grain trucks, pickups (there were only a few in the county when I was a youth), wagons, and four-wheeled, rubber-tired trailers pulled by cars or tractors began arriving at the stock-yard at sunrise with the lambs for shipping. Some lambs even arrived in the back of the family cars. Cars were not just to ride in; they doubled as a pickup before a second vehicle could be afforded. Shipping day was a very interesting display of grassroots mid-America just escaping the Depression days. There was a medley of bleating, yelling, tractor noise, and barking for background effects as kids, wives, neighbors, and dogs helped the transfer of lambs to the enclosure on the scales.

In the pen, the lambs were weighed and graded for quality. After that, they were herded up a ramp into the rail cars. The noise was fascinating. Everyone hollered with different words in a different pitch of voice. This human noise mixed with barking of dogs and bleating of the lambs was to be heard throughout this little hamlet until the shipping was concluded just before noon.

The farmers were all in a hurry, as it was spring and everyone had fieldwork waiting. Several men helped push a trailer to the unloading chute while the owner took his tractor or car out of the way so someone else could move into position. Another reason to grade and weigh the lambs quickly was the fact farmers were paid by the weight of the lambs shipped. A trailer of waiting and excited lambs could urinate away a few dollars!

The County Agent and his shepherd friend were qualified by the packinghouse to grade the lambs for proper payment. Lambs with backs that felt like a board were graded number one and were given a circle of blue paint on their back. When the lamb's backbone and ribs could be felt, the red circle denoting second rating was applied to the lamb's back. Quite often these seconds were taken home to be fed more grain and be brought back the next shipping day, two weeks later. By the time the last lamb was loaded into the freight car, these men had multicolored trousers and smelled like shearers.

We kids crawled onto the railroad cars and played train if we were not old enough to help with the transfer process. It must have been as close as we got to the excitement city kids experienced when the circus came to town.

A few hours after the lambs were loaded, a Rock Island train stopped for the cars that contained the lambs, and then headed to Kansas City. Marion County had a Spring Lamb reputation for quite a while.

Coyotes and dog packs caused problems for the flock owners. It was not unusual to find a sheep killed by a coyote. If we found it while still alive, we had a choice: we could doctor it or we could kill it to salvage what could be used for food.

Not everyone in the community learned to eat lamb. I was gardening when a car roared up the road beside our farm. I heard the tires skiding on the road gravel as it came over the hill. Our fat lambs had found their way onto the road and a neighbor was sliding into them. Seven or eight fat lambs were dead or badly hurt. We quickly butchered them and froze most of the meat.

Later in the week we went to a Sunday school picnic. We roasted a lot of lamb and took it to the picnic on a large platter. One of the fellows came to my wife with his plate nearly empty and said, "Jacquie, I hear you fixed that good platter of veal. It is sure tasty."

"Wes," she said, "that's not veal, its lamb!"

He looked at her, made a beeline to the restroom, and lost his meal!

Andy started this sheep chapter so let's close with him. One afternoon Dad went to the south eighty for hay. He noticed the sheep out in the spring wheat, and then some unexplained activity caught his eye. When he finished loading the hay, he went to investigate. As he got closer he could see the ram thrashing around and his dad, Andy, then in his seventies, on the ground hanging onto the ram's neck for dear life.

After Dad ran the ram off he asked Grandpa, "What happened?"

"Dat damn ram tried to till me!"

"What were you doing?"

"Dem sheep vas eatin in von place onle so I came out and ven I raised my arms to shoo dem somevhere else, dat dam ram came fer me."

Louis did not tell his dad that raised hands were his signal for "it's playtime."

Trains stayed around longer than the buggies, but why aren't there any depots now? What happened to the section hands and the local stockyards?

Chapter 12

Travel, a Problem?

It Depending on the Weather

Harness the horses and get the surrey
Grab a horse blanket, your mittens too
If we get to church we'll have to hurry
Or there'll be no empty pew.

The surrey may be idealistic. It seems bankers used these two-seated horse drawn carriages, while most other people used the cheaper one-seated buggy.

Still others used a produce wagon with a spring seat that reached across its top to rest on both sides. Produce was transported to town in the spring wagon, often called a box wagon or lumber wagon. These wagons used two horses instead of the one horse needed for some buggies.

Since there were no garages, buggies were kept in the barns or granaries. One time when Dad was a boy, he was up in the hayloft and slipped. He fell onto the taut canvas buggy top below and bounced to the ground, sustaining less injury than if he had hit the ground directly.

Hitching rails were installed at schools for kids who rode a horse or a buggy to school. These convenient rails were also available at churches and along main streets.

For long distance travel, such as a trip to conduct business in the next county or two away or to visit relatives several towns away, people rode the fast steam trains. These noisy iron giants fascinated me, as they did other country boys. The noise and smell could not be topped. It was fun to stand near the tracks and wave at the engineers as they passed.

It was always fun to run to the tracks after church in Aulne to watch the station agent tie a mail sack to the pickup tower beside the track. A man on the train's mail car would swing outward a steel arm and grab the sack as the train roared through town at full speed. One of my favorite sounds was the whistle of a steam locomotive as it approached road crossings at every mile, especially on a cold clear winter night when the sound carried well. A long plume of black smoke followed the engine, a sight to see in the daytime.

Just as the farm scenes were changing, the railroads did too. Trains shifted from steam to diesel. The smoke disappeared, and the diesel engine's horn was not as romantic as the whistle of the steam locomotive.

Several miles south of the Larsen farm was the Santa Fe main line, which ran between Chicago and Los Angeles. The two sets of tracks carried a lot of transcontinental passenger trains. It is reported that up to six or so passenger trains serviced our towns daily. A number of the steam-engine passenger trains could stop in all the little towns in the county, as did the freight trains. Often they were stopped by the station master waving a flag indicating there was a passenger. But the fast streamliners with brightly painted diesel engines would pull down on the horn and charge full speed through town. They only stopped at the larger cities. Before airlines, important national figures and movie stars used these most modern of trains to travel between coasts. Celebraties would ride The Chief, The Super Chief, or The El Capitan streamliners between Los Angeles and Chicago before the airlines developed commercially.

A secondary branch track of the Santa Fe passed through Marion. Its passenger service was limited to a one-car unit called the DoodleBug, which traveled rather slowly across several counties. As the state became populated the Santa Fe developed many branch lines.

The town of Florence had a Harvey House for good meals before dining cars became available. Fred Harvey arranged with the Santa Fe to operate these eating establishments at regular distances along its line. Girls with good character and an eighth-grade education were hired with a promise of six months of employment if they maintained certain standards, including staying single. They set a standard for waitresses to come. Fortunately, this historical site in Florence remains and can be toured today.

The Rock Island Railroad was the second rail line in the county running in a north to south direction connecting Marion, Aulne, and Peabody as it moved from Herrington to Wichita. The line was quite busy in the early nineteen hundreds. Their crack streamliner was the Rocket, which hit its top speed on a set of straight track south of Aulne. This line suffered from the economic woes of the mid-century and its tide all but ebbed to a close. There has been a turn around and the line with a new name is now again in operation.

There were several train wrecks in the county. Dad and I witnessed a passenger train hit a livestock truck in Peabody. Fortunately, the truck had almost crossed the tracks when it was hit. It took the train a quarter of a mile to come to a stop. After the train had gone by, the big truck chassis sat parallel to the tracks and the truck bed and livestock racks were scattered along the right-of-way.

One of my fellow students in high school was killed in Marion as she crossed the tracks and didn't hear a train. When I was teaching in Peabody, a tramp walking into town on the tracks did not hear a train. He was killed beside the school playground while our students were playing during the lunch hour. The lunch period ended abruptly!

Freight for stores or farms came into the depot freight room, and produce went out by train as well. The depot in Peabody had an overhanging roof so buggies could drive under it for unloading in rainy weather. Both Marion and Peabody had two depots. At least twelve depots served the county in the years when the population was growing. Now only one exists in the county. Marion bought its Santa Fe depot and later converted it to the city library.

The railroads started reducing their rural assets shortly after midcentury. Each town, including little Aulne, had a series of houses for the section gang – the crew that maintained the tracks. Just as on the farm, mechanization did away with need for these crews years ago, and the houses are gone. The stock-loading yards have also disappeared, and livestock is now moved in huge trucks. Arnold Burns, a large cattle feeder, used to bring a trainload of cattle into Peabody from Texas for fattening on a regular basis. Texas cattle would arrive in the Flint Hills east of us by train for summer grazing.

One seldom sees livestock cars on the rails now. The railroad tide was ebbing, but would not disappear.

The early surge in population required counties to bridge the streams. Now some of the counties can no longer afford to maintain bridges properly, which forces some school buses to be routed away from questionable spans.

Country roads were surveyed, marked, and developed in the early years, but they remained dirt, dust, and mud. Later the national highway system became established. U. S. Highway 50, which eventually became a transcontinental highway, was built in pieces and stages as roads in different states were connected. Kansas authorized its part of construction in 1931. It came by the Larsen farmhouse as a sanded road. Now Dad or Mother could drive to town on rainy days, while neighbors would have to wait for their dirt roads to dry, or travel in deep ruts if the rains continued.

There was not a lot of traffic on the highway when I was a kid. Most of the few vehicles were older cars. There were only a few pickups. Most hauling was by horse and wagon or by a four-wheel trailer made from an old car chassis and pulled by the family car. When rubber-tired tractors with a road-speed gear became available, they did a lot of the hauling.

Several times I was able to stand by our fence by the road and watch the Army's cavalry troops ride by on a trip from Fort Riley near Junction City. Another sight became somewhat regular during World War II. Houses for defense workers in Wichita were hauled down the highway by large moving trucks.

Early farmers received compensation from the county government to maintain the county dirt roads often called section roads. This meant using a simple implement called a road drag to knock down the clods and fill ruts, as well as keeping ditches free of weeds with a mowing machine. Later, the county took over the grading task. One crewman could grade dozens of miles of road and do a better job. The relieved farmers now could attend to other duties. The Larsen road drag rests in a hedgerow and has not been used since. A half-century later this action would earn the term, downsizing, a word meaning the tide was ebbing and jobs were being lost. Several decades later a few of the more-used side roads were graveled to make them passable in wet weather.

One wet year when I was a child, I had a part in the church Christmas Eve children's program. The family started for church in the Model T. Dad couldn't get the car wheels out of the ruts. It was slow going. By the time the family arrived in Aulne, the program had been in progress for quite some time and would soon be over. Dad was able to turn around on the better road in town and we went home. Phyllis and I were disappointed to miss any gifts under the church Christmas tree; however, a battery radio at home brought the Christmas Eve church programs to us.

One might think that with the cheap Model T and gas at two cents per gallon, people would do a lot of traveling. But with hogs selling at only one and a half to two cents per pound, we didn't have much money to buy gas. The farmer had two sets of gas barrels: one for the car and another for the first tractor he had just purchased. Tractor gasoline sold for a half cent less than car gas, since it required no road tax.

In the midcentury, the highway system was upgraded, which changed the routes dramatically. This time large machines formed the roadbed instead of teams of horses and Fresno slips. Rather than go through small towns, highways skirted them by as much as a mile or more. Instead of following section lines as in the past, U.S. 50 South was rerouted to parallel to the Santa Fe railroad tracks, cutting through all the dozen sections of land between Florence and Peabody, except two.

Farmers became furious but couldn't do anything about their frustration. "Pete can't get from one part of his field to the next without going to the east corner, up the road to cross the highway, and then back west to enter his other ten acres!"

These highways made it much easier for trucks, and soon a big increase in their number matched the decline in the number of trains needed, an example of opposing tides. Thus, only one Santa Fe track remains on the right-of-way instead of the two sets of the past. Shipping of milk and cream, as well as livestock, left the railcars for the more convenient trucks. The railroads slipped into an ebb tide as rural freight and passenger demands dwindled.

Airplanes arrived on the scene much later. Air routes, like highways and railroads, changed, bypassing formerly important places. At one time, Wichita called itself the air capital of the nation, because it was an important refueling stop for planes traveling across the country. Such travel was not called trans-continental yet. Then planes were developed with larger fuel capacity, which meant they didn't land for fuel as often. Transcontinental planes have rendered Wichita no longer necessary as a major air traffic hub.

The Larsen farm was near the flyway between Kansas City and Wichita, so we did see a few planes or hear them struggling along in the adolescent days of flight. The early rotary gasoline engines could be heard approaching miles away. Sighting these planes was easy, but spotting the first jets was difficult, as the plane was way ahead of its sound. We had to recalibrate our mental sensing equipment.

On clear nights we would go outside upon hearing the nightly mail plane. We would try to find its lights amongst the stars. A network of airplane beacons was strung between Kansas City and Wichita to mark the night route before electronic navigation. On a clear night as a boy, I could follow the line of rotating lights located in the counties south of the farm.

When Wichita airplane plants geared up for World War II, we would see flights of completed planes flying northeastward. Uncle Roy and Aunt Evie were the only people we knew who had been in an airplane. My Uncle Roy had his own! As a boy, I found airplanes interesting. I would draw racing planes and biplanes when finished with my eighth grade arithmetic assignments. Plane wheels weren't retractable so they were enclosed in a closed fender similar to that of some motorcycles. I drew such fenders and colored them red. We boys never thought we would ever be lucky or rich enough to fly in an airplane. Would the young airline industries' tide come in?

Farming was work that seemed to never be finished. Was there any way to escape it for an hour of so, other than going to school or church? Would there ever be much fun for farm kids?

Chapter 13

Saturday Nights
Social Life And Shopping

The dull plowshares go to Oliver the Smithy
And cream and eggs to Bob's Cream Station.
We'll get black shoe polish to look spiffy
And a can pork and beans for our ration.

On Saturday night we would go to either Marion or Peabody with a can or two of cream, each holding five or ten gallons, as well as our fifteen or thirty dozen cases of eggs. Leaving town for home, we would pick up the empty and washed cream cans. It was nice to have a car with an attached trunk above the rear bumper. Not all of the produce had to ride between the seats.

As we arrived in town on Saturday night, Mother would say, "Louis, stop at the cream station before you go to the blacksmith's. I'll get the advance cream and egg money so I won't have to wait while you talk to Oliver. I can get started shopping."

Mother, like other farm wives, tried to make the egg and cream money cover purchases she made in town. A neighbor to the west, Mrs. Freesauger, always put ten percent of her cream-station money, her tithe for church the next morning, in a separate coin purse. Bookkeeping and accounting were simple. There were no credit cards to juggle and manage.

Mother and my sister got out of the car and started for the stores to do the shopping. Now it was on to the blacksmith's shop for Dad and me, to drop off a set or two of dull plow shares and pick up the ones left several days ago for sharpening. The share is the cutting edge of the plow. After slicing miles of soil, the cutting edge becomes worn and dull. We would unbolt this heavy, thick piece of the metal and take it to a blacksmith to be sharpened with his forge and an anvil.

On Saturday nights, Oliver Kornhaus, the smithy, was dressed in clean clothes and was in a jovial mood; it was payday for him. There was no sweat on his wide brow. "Oliver, I brought you two sets of shares," Dad would say and then ask, "Is the set I left last week sharpened and ready?"

"Yeah, but I wish it would rain," Oliver would reply. This stocky, short man would mutter, "Wish some of you farmers would go fishin' now and then so I could catch up on the work. You farmers are dulling your shares too fast. I can't keep up with you guys."

"I don't think that's it," Dad would answer. "With bigger tractors pulling three bottom plows instead of two, we're ganging up on you. Some of us have put lights on our tractors and are putting in more hours of plowing a day. With a boy at home we can keep it going longer."

Oliver had an equally short and stocky brother who had his own smithy several blocks away and was Oliver's competition.

As a boy, I found it much more interesting to visit the blacksmith shop in the daytime when the belts and pulleys of the jack shaft overhead were moving noisily. There was a pulley over each of his machines: grinders, buffers, a drophammer, a drill press, and a fan for the forge. Moving a lever hanging beside the jack shaft engaged the pulley running a belt to the machine.

It was exciting to watch the spray of red-hot sparks that flew from the grinding wheel. The pyrotechnics, the noise, the half barrel of sizzling water, which created steam as hot iron was dropped into it - everything was fascinating. I would watch as Oliver, with sweat on his face, lifted his foot off the circle of pipe that activated the huge belt-driven drop hammer to pound an orange-hot shear thinner into a cutting edge. The smell of the forge was different from the farm smells I was accustomed to.

Oliver doused the shear into a keg of water again before placing it back into the forge for more heat. Then he nudged more coals onto the fire and removed a second red-hot shear ready for hammering. Oliver was lucky here in mid-century as he had the drop hammer to pound the steel. The smithy who sharpened Andy's shears had only the forge, a heavy hammer, and an anvil.

John Deere was given the credit for developing the steel plow that made it possible to convert the prairie into tillable soil. The blacksmith should be given credit for keeping the plow sharp. Before the days of electrical power to run the jackshaft, the smithy had to pound the hot plowshare into a new edge by arm power. He did not need to go to a gym to stay fit. He also had to forge hot pieces of metal together for many other repairs before gas or electric welders were available. A smith was a professional fixer of many heavy items, but unfortunately he gets credit for mainly shoeing horses.

Other towns had blacksmith shops and even Aulne, just a crossroads community now, had a blacksmith in its heyday. Lou Chapman was remembered for two reasons. He was one of the first to buy an acetylene welder. Not only was the use of his welder a fascinating process to watch, but he practiced what everyone thought was a dumb idea: he welded on top of a barrel of gasoline. "As long as the barrel is full of gasoline, there's no problem," he would say. "I don't want to weld on top of a barrel containing gasoline fumes!" He must have been right, as he later retired alive, but he never had many clients stand and watch him weld their broken iron.

His second feat was driving his kids to high school using his own gasoline. "Yup, I go to my well and pump a barrel of water, wait an hour or so and skim off gasoline." A filling station's underground tank had developed a leak and polluted all of Aulne's wells except one. Everyone had to carry water for drinking and cooking from the town's one good well.

No one remembered to share this problem to the new minister's wife. For the first meal she prepared after moving in, she started boiling potatoes over a gas stove and the potatoes were blown around the kitchen. Also, no one told her which outhouse behind the church was for which sex, as the parishioners all knew. When she found out, she cured any doubts any visitors might have: she painted MEN and NO MEN on the appropriate doors.

When we had the blacksmith business out of the way, there were other things to do in town on a Saturday night. This was the time to get a haircut if a family did not have their own haircutter. We men would make a quick walk up one side of the street and down the other to see which of the barbers had the shortest waiting line. Hair cutting might last until ten at night or later.

Saturday night was a social time as well as a shopping trip. You could fall in line with a friend or a relative and visit while walking the sidewalk and checking the various specials advertised in the store windows. On warm evenings the sidewalk could be crowded. Men would lean against a car or sit on a fender and visit with each other: crops, livestock, or gossip about someone else. Kids who weren't in tow with their parents would play tag or other games. One boy who had suffered from a polio bout had shriveled legs. His thighs were the size of his wrists, but he could run and play tag on his crutches. What shoulders that boy had!

There was a lot to talk about on the way home, as everyone in the car had something to share. However, if the game of tag lasted very long, the kids were asleep in a mile or two, as car speeds rarely exceeded thirty miles per hour on the dirt roads. "Ruth said the Danskins are retiring and moving to town after the corn is shucked. They bought the little house on Olive Street next to the highway." Or, "Guess where Bill and Ella are moving?" Since landowners might change tenants every year or two, there was a lot of moving and that was news in midwinter. March 1 was the starting and ending date for rental farms. For years, this meant loading things into a hayrack or lumberwagon and calling, "Gitty up." There were a lot of rural address changes each March.

Many people living in town avoided the business area on Saturday afternoon and night, not because they had anything against farmers, they just wanted to avoid crowds. Not only was parking a problem, being waited on was a problem in a crowded store. Stores in the thirties were not self-service; you needed a clerk. Two or three clerks would be in line as you entered a grocery store. The one at the head of the line with a basket in hand would step forward and ask, "Can I help you?"

"Yes, please."

"What would you like?"

"A can of crushed pineapple, black shoe polish, a box of matches, some mustard and a sack of flour."

"A fifty pound sack?"

"Yes, and a sack of sugar, a bar of baking chocolate," and the list went on. There was little canned fruit, meat, or vegetables as a rule in the farm wife's sack of groceries, other than an occasional can of pineapple or salmon. A treat would be a little sack of candy.

As the clerk put the groceries in the basket he was carrying, he jotted down the item onto a pad he carried, using a carbon paper to make a copy as he wrote. When the shopper finished, the clerk escorted her to the counter near the door. There the owner took the clerk's list, added up the bill, bagged the groceries with the list carbon, and took the patron's cash.

Other than at grocery stores, merchandise was wrapped with brown paper and tied with sting. Often the paper had tinted paisley watermark-like patterns, which children loved to follow like a maze with a pencil or crayon when the package was emptied. In a shop a spool of string rested somewhere out of the way. Its string rose to the high embossed tin ceiling, passing through several screw eyes placed to allow the string's end to hang where the shopkeeper could reach it above him to tie any packages. It was a fascinating round-and-round wrapping motion, a hocus-pocus of the hands, and a snap as the string flipped around a finger to be parted with a pull.

Before the era of the supermarket, meat was purchased at a separate butchershop. Since farm families had their own canned or smoked meat, farm wives bought only peanut butter in such shops. Peanut butter was kept in large waxed paper lined-boxes in the butcher's case. "How much do you want?" the butcher asked.

"Two pounds if it's fresh. If it's not, a pound is enough."

"It just came in on the train yesterday!" With a large wooden paddle he scooped out several slabs of peanut butter and placed them into a white cardboard boat. After he put the boat on the large, white Toledo scales, he either added or subtracted until the right amount registered.

The paper, this time white instead of brown, was pulled from a roll and again the string routine. The butcher then pulled a black grease pencil from behind his ear and marked the price on the package. A wife knew how fresh the peanut butter was by the time she got home. A fresh product had grease stains showing on the outside wrapper, whereas the stale stuff still had a clean boat. Incidentally, chunky peanut butter had not made its appearance. It didn't appear until the last half of the century.

Another first stop for men had to be the implement store to

purchase a box of sickle sections for the mower, a new canvas for the grain binder, or other needed repairs or parts.

Since our farm was between Marion and Peabody, we did not always go to the same town for repairs and groceries. Our destination often depended on which implement dealer had the necessary machine part Dad needed.

Routines and pecking orders were established. Some people arrived at Main Street at a "usual" time that was a routine for them. This did not work well for Ross, a cocky little fellow who lived a mile or so west of town. He started losing a few chickens from the chicken house each Saturday night. One Saturday, after driving to his usual parking area in the late afternoon, he and his wife walked the street as always. Then he told his wife, "Let's go home and see if we have company." Sure enough, they had been seen in town by a neighbor and his wife who were now in Ross's chicken house gathering chickens. The fellow needed to sell a few chickens for money to purchase peanut butter.

Ross got his gun and told the neighbor, "Let's walk to town."

After a quarter of a mile, the neighbor pleaded, "My wife has bad feet and can't walk any further."

"Pick up that damn woman and carry her!" was Ross's response.

A farmer did not have to listen to the Dow Jones report to know about the economy. Instead, he listened to the farm market reports early in the morning before chores and at noon to hear what grain or stock would bring if he shipped that day. When chicken stealing occurred, times were getting tough. In good times stealing didn't happen.

Not only were there apartments over the stores, there were a number of shops in basements: a barber, a shoemaker, a sewing machine repair man and others with an appropriate window and door at the foot of stone steps. Each town also had a movie theater. Now there is not a theater in the county. Theaters have joined the milk trains and the hired man in the out-washing tide.

One reads that the pioneers were prudes and upright people. Was there no fun? What could several big boys do for excitement? What about fireworks that continued to bang as repeaters? Were there no pranks?

Chapter 14

High Jinks and Orneriness

Beware

Some folks are a tease, and just for fun.
They cause not trouble, but just drop a pun.
Others are ornery and don't always play fair.
They've done their deed; you know they've been there.

When my parents were adolescents, with no commercial amusements of note, a lot of interaction developed between boys. Tricks and stunts almost became a way of life. Many were a harmless form of teasing.

Mother's twin brothers, Earnest and Earl Winkley, wrapped a mailing tube with red paper and attached a white twine in one end. After Christmas dinner they coaxed cousin Sylvester to help them light this firecracker. While he and one of the twins lit the fuse and ran around the barn, the other twin fired off a shotgun. Running to see the hole it blew in the ground, they found the firecracker unexploded, so they lit it again before once more running behind a shed. Who had the most fun?

Another time one of the twins sat by Sylvester at Christmas dinner and put whipped cream on Sylvester's pork and beans, much to the disgust of several proper ladies present. Sylvester thought it a good idea and took another serving of beans. Again he had assistance with whipped cream from his cousin. No harm done, but a lot of fun for a roomful of people and a memory for decades.

Boys have always hung a swing over a creek to drop in for the fun of a "big splash." The Hett boys did this and then went one better.

During World War II, a movie short subject showed pictures of adolescents in Florida having a lot of fun on boards pulled behind motorboats in Cypress Gardens. "Hey, we could do that," one of the boys said.

The next Sunday, while the parents were at a funeral, the boys removed a door from a sheep barn and parked a tractor at a bend in the creek. Slipping a five-gallon paint bucket wound with electric fence wire onto the tractor's belt pulley, they were ready. They unwound the smooth wire and pulled it to a point along the end or the straight part of the creek. There they attached it to the barn door and put the door into the water. A little rope served as handle for the rider. On a signal, the boy on the tractor put the pulley into gear and reeled in the wire. What a hydroplane and what cheap, exciting fun! However, one time the boy on the tractor forgot to push in the clutch causing the rider to all but crash onto the tractor.

In the early part of the twentieth Century, "Old Man Kush" had a butcher shop in Aulne. He closed on Memorial Day and painted the floor of his shop. His sons found several baby rabbits in a hay field that was being mowed. "Hey, we'll take the bunnies back to town," they decided. "We can keep them in Dad's store." They slipped the bunnies in the door of the butcher shop. Next morning when Kush opened the door he saw a lot of tracks in his new paint job. "Oh, dem Got damn raats, I chust as soon live as to die!"

Another time several men were seining fish on Catlin Creek when they looked up and saw someone coming. Could it be a game warden? Pulling the seine out of the creek, they began to run away. Kush got his feet tangled in the seine and fell. "Ruhn poys, ruhn fer your life. Dey got ole Kush!" The stranger turned out to be someone looking for a fishing hole.

This story is not a trick, but it was too unbelievable to forget. One day after church was over, the Hett boys told about Dr. Branch, a dentist on the edge of Aulne. It just wasn't believable, but you should believe a doctor. Doc and the Hetts shared a common pasture fence. After a summer thunderstorm, both were checking to see that the fence was still in good condition. "Hey, Doc," the boys said, "our dad says you registered those dogs you raise. Does that mean you have papers on them?

"Yes, you bet I do."

"How come?

"It is a way of keeping track of their parentage and descendants to keep the Boston Bull bloodline correct. That is how a breed remains pure. Both parents must have papers as purebreds before the puppies can be registered with the national organizations."

The boys thought about that while Doc took a pull on his pipe. That pipe also caught the boys' attention. Sunday school teachers had taught them that smoking was a sin. Pop Hett had stressed that it was dangerous for farmers to smoke around dry crops and barns.

"Doc, does anybody ever buy a registered Boston Bull?" All farm boys knew that dogs were free. You didn't even have to ask for one, as someone always wanted to give away a puppy or two.

"Yeah," Doc said, thrusting his chin and pipe outward. "Matter of fact, the other day a fellow from California called about a dog." Now he really had the boys fascinated. No one used long distance calls except to report a death or birth in the extended family. That guy in California was as crazy as Doc: wanting to buy a dog, calling long distance about it, and during hard times!

"Did he buy a dog?"

"Well, he wanted me to give him a better description of the one I had advertised in our national *Boston Bull* magazine."

Now Doc was the crazy one, spending money to advertise a dog. "What happened? Did he really want the dog?"

"Well, he said it sounded like a good dog and asked how much I wanted for it."

"How much did ja want?"

"I said, a hundred dollars."

At that time, not only did farmers not have registered cows, they didn't have to pay a hundred dollars for one. This conversation was getting to be unbelievable. "What did he say to that, Doc? Did he hang up?"

"He asked if I didn't have a better dog."

"Did ja?"

"No, I just described the same dog using longer words. I also paused longer between sentences like I was admiring him. Then he asked what I wanted for the dog. I told him he was my personal dog and I hadn't planned on selling him. I patted my leg hard enough for the phone to pick up the sound-effects noise, like I was patting the dog."

Now the boys knew Doc was beyond help, turning down a

hundred dollars for a dog. Before the boys could say more, Doc went on, "'How much would it take to part with him?' the Californian asked." The boys knew this was getting to be a lengthy long distance call. It must by now be over the three-minute mark, which meant over-time would be charged. "It would have to be at least two hundred before I would consider letting him go. He's like family."

"What'd he say then?"

"'Ship him.' the guy said." This story impressed the Hett boys, and they had a homegrown fable to tell the rest of us the next morning after church. Doc picked up his fence-fixing tools and headed for his farmstead on the outskirts of Aulne. Perhaps he had to fix someone's teeth in his home office.

This conversation took place in the early thirties, when Kansas was suffering from not only the Great Depression but also a long-lasting drought. My parents had given up on their teeth, but although they could afford to have them pulled, they didn't have enough money for dentures. So they went a year without teeth. No one used credit in those days: it was "cash and carry" or, in this case, cash and pull! Mother pounded beefsteak a lot before she fried it so they could eat it. They also had a lot of fresh, homemade bread, potatoes, and gravy that year.

A chivaree was a folk ritual of tricks played on a newly married couple as an initiation to married life. Planning took place a week or so after the wedding, and hopefully, the event could be held on an evening after a rain, so fieldwork did not have to be compromised. The word would go out: "Chivaree for Elsie and Ed tonight at 9:30. Meet at the corner east of their house." The party announcements never need-ed to tell anyone what to do; everyone brought all the noisemakers they could find. Wives had big spoons to pound upon the old pans they brought. Kids brought their current version of a noisemaker.

One popular noisemaker was the tic-tack. The homemade device consisted of a long string tied to a nail. The prankster shoved the nail between any of the exterior boards on the house, then pulled the string quite tight. When he plucked the string, a weird, loud noise resonated inside the house. You thought you were inside a base violin.

Some man would bring his bull fiddle. A bull fiddle was a home-constructed device made of a large metal gear. A crank turned the gear against a metal strap. Several men placed and held the device against the side of a house as another turned the crank; the noise inside could be deafening.

Everyone hooted, called, and howled for the couple to come out. When they finally did, it was customary to congratulate them and share the candy, popcorn, or whatever refreshments the couple had prepared to serve at this expected impromptu ritual.

Generally the process stopped here, but sometimes the couple would be separated for the evening, or both would be taken to town, where the new husband would push his wife down Main Street in a wheelbarrow with everyone following with car horns blaring.

Looking forward to a chivaree was rather frightening to a young couple. The house they had fixed up that could be dirtied with muddy feet, they could be separated, and there might be unexpected tricks. Having the bed short sheeted or filled with cornflakes was expected, as people wandered through the house to see how the newlyweds had fixed it up! The couple would let the pranksters honk and hoot, but it made good sense to come out before they could start playing tricks in the yard. A chivaree was Halloween on call whenever necessary. Once chivareed, the couple was an accepted neighbor in the community.

Dad was as tricky as anyone was. Ole Stub, his dog, loved to fetch sticks and Louis would accommodate him. Stub knew to watch Dad and his playfulness. The stick would often land near a ewe with a new lamb. When it did Stub seemed to be thinking, "Is my master using me to check the reflexes of the ewe? Could he be setting me up to get into trouble? Its hard to tell."

One winter morning I walked across the road to my parents' place to start chores. I noticed there were no tracks in the snow leading from the house so Dad wasn't outside yet. As I opened the back door to check in, I nearly went through the ceiling. I was looking into the face of a raccoon at eye level! Stub and Dad had killed a raccoon during the night. When he saw me coming, my father placed the frozen animal on a box of wood on the back porch. He then hid to watch the surprise.

One of his stunts backfired. Dad trained a bucket calf to butt his knee. One day when she was about five, my sister Phyllis was playing in the yard near the calf, which decided it needed more butting practice. She screamed loudly. Mom rescued her and Dad received an ultimatum that evening: "You keep that calf in the corral, do you hear?"

Not all tricks happened on Louis's watch, and not all boys came out of church with a nice attitude. "Hey, guys," the Hett boys or I would yell, "let's do Albert's Model A again."

"Yeah, I'll get the block of wood," another of us answered.

Albert was a bachelor uncle to the seven Hett boys. This well-liked fellow in his thirties was at church every Sunday with Bible in hand. While we boys were outside as soon as possible, Albert, like the other adults, liked to visit with other parishioners. This gap of time was sufficient for us to do our trick. Meanwhile, Albert's sister Ruby would find Albert and ask, "Albert, why don't you come over for dinner," which is what we called the noon meal in that locale.

"I'll come. I'll bring the children with me," he replied meaning Ruby's boy and girl.

By that time one of us boys had retrieved a block of wood from last week's hiding place. He gave us the word: "Ok, guys, lift 'er up." The rest of us took a grip on the rear bumper of this lightweight Model A coupe.

"Higher guys," we were commanded. Then, "Let 'er down now." With the block under the under the left axle, the wheel was just off the ground.

"Let's go! He's coming!" It was a dash with heads down to hide behind other parked cars to enjoy the fun. We all had smiles and smirks.

With his niece and nephew safely in the coupe, Albert was ready. He started the car, put it into gear, and looked over his shoulder before starting to back out onto the street.

"He's going to try it," the tricksters snickered from a safe distance. The wheel in the air began to move but Albert and the car did not budge. "Look, he's shifted into low and is trying to go forward," and we elbowed each other and laughed harder. "Now he's getting out to see what's wrong!"

Next Sunday the process would be repeated, as Albert never thought to look under the car before getting into it, or to take the block with him after he had pushed the car off it. "Get the block and hide it. We can use it next week," one of us would say, and we hid it again.

If this was the way boys acted on Sunday, what did they do on Halloween? Could they be tolerated? Have all the memories faded?

Chapter 15

Halloweens Past
What an Excuse for Fun!

"Trick or treat, trick or treat!"
Call the little folk from the street.
But it's the stunts of bigger boys
That are pulled without the noise.

Years ago Halloween was not a holiday just for little folks. Many stories were told by Dad of the horse-and-buggy day's version of what the "big boys" did on Halloween. It was always interesting to see who was the subject of their pranks. Homeowners with an interesting idiosyncrasy usually received a stunt or two on a yearly basis. I don't think Dad was in on many, if any, of the pranks in his stories. At least, he never owned up to any.

Madsen, a young bachelor, on the morning after Halloween, often found his buggy had been taken around the block and parked on a maiden lady's front lawn. One year the boys came down his alley to move it again. "Hey, Joe, you be the horse, act like a trotter, and we'll all push from behind." Joe took a shaft in each hand and turned the buggy into the alley. It was a clear night and a downhill jaunt to the park where the boys were planning to leave it this year.

"Ok," Joe replied, "I'll head for the park. We kin leave it on the race track." Picking up the buggy shafts, he turned toward the street.

As the boys and buggy entered the park, the horse blanket in the buggy moved and Mr. Madsen sat up with his shotgun. "Joe, it's time to go back to the house," he ordered. It took a little longer to get the buggy back up the hill and put in its place beside the horse barn. "I hope you boys enjoyed the trip tonight," Mr. Madsen said as he went in his back door, "and don't come back, as I'm going to stay awake."

The boys went on down the alley muttering, "And don't come back, I'll be awake." They found other tricks to perform, but the buggy owner had set himself up for further attention. When the boys came back that way an hour later, they noticed his light was out. They found and disconnected the tin cans he had attached under the buggy to awaken him if the boys did return.

Instead, the young fellow was awakened next morning when the marshal called to ask, "Hey, Madsen, are you missing a buggy this morning? There's one on top of Smith's barn north of town that looks like yours. I drove down the alley and yours isn't where you usually park it."

Before the days of indoor toilets, boys would run down the alleys at Halloween night and wreak havoc by tipping over outhouses, one after another. No damage was done, but the next morning when the family needed a privy in a hurry, it did take a moment before satisfaction could occur. Until theirs could be righted, the family had to find a neighbor whose unit was still standing and use that one, much to the chuckles of others. Some families planted rosebushes around the outhouse which helped protect it.

Husbands and fathers were expected to guard against this prank. One older man, who had needed help to right his outhouse the mornings after Halloween, decided to prevent it happening again. He took his shotgun into the outhouse as it got dark and prepared to confront the pranksters. He spent an hour or so practicing his confrontation: "Not tonight, boys! You got me last year; it's someone else's turn. Call it a night, boys. Go home."

"It's a nightmare," he thought as he pitched forward and felt himself falling. The nightmare ended as quickly as it started as he realized he had fallen asleep and the boys had won again. The boys too were surprised to hear a plaintive call from the overturned structure, "Boys, boys, de door ish down! 'Elp me please!"

Another time an apprentice tipper paid heavily for his first tipping experience, a real initiation to the ritual. "Can I go with you big guys? I got enough candy and I want to go with you, please!" Now the "big guys" had experience and knew the dangers and pitfalls of the tipping business. They brought a pole along to start the tipping process. Young Jimmy had not yet seen the pole in use. High on sugar from the trick-or-treat candy he had eaten and wanting to show he could help, he bolted ahead, to the back of Schmidt's privy. Schmidt had been visited by these boys in the past, and unbeknownst to Jimmy, had prepared for any visits tonight. On a full run, with his hands raised to start the pushover, Jimmy looked up instead of down and fell into the pit. Jake Schmidt had moved his privy forward several feet.

"Help me out, I keep sliding back into it," Jimmy pleaded as he grasped the pole extended to him. He didn't get much sympathy for awhile as the big boys leaned on each other laughing and giving thanks it wasn't them. "I can't go home this way, what'll I do?"

One of the boys remembered that a neighbor had a hydrant by his carriage barn. "Come on, I'll hose you off at Snider's barn."

The plan was carried out, but it was not an altogether happy solution. "Hey, the water's ice cold," Jimmy cried.

"Wait a minute till the water in the hose is gone. The water in the pipes below ground will be warmer. Now, is that better? Turn around and I'll wash your backside."

"But the wind makes me cold."

Another boy approached. "I found this gunny sack out behind. Get out of your clothes and slip it on. I've cut a hole in it for your head. Kick your clothes and shoes over in the weeds. You can get them tomorrow after school."

"Yeah, but my shoes are new!"

"Suit yourself, you still smell."

"I'm goin' home."

After school the next day, Jimmy stopped at the grocery store for two paper sacks, one to hold his clothes and one to put his hand into while retrieving the clothes and shoes. But when he reached the weedy where his clothes should have been, they were gone. "Where's my clothes? They ain't here where I kicked 'em last night!"

Two people did know where the clothes were. As Schmidt came out to push his outhouse back where it belonged, he had met Palmer the trashman coming up the alley making his rounds.

"Hey, looks like boys pushed your privy ahead last night as a prank! Oh, these kids!"

"Nope, they get me each year, so this time I moved it forward to reverse the stunt. Hey, it worked, one fell in!"

"That explains the pile of dirty clothes I found up the alley. They stunk, so I threw them into my wagon. I'll bet we never find out who it was. If I were that kid, I wouldn't tell either!"

After hearing several of these stories, I knew why my relatives waited until I was older and beyond such foolishness to relate them to me. I noticed a certain glimmer in the eyes of uncles as they related the stories between bouts of laughter.

It had been a great evening for the special effects of celebration. The full moon had crawled above the eastern horizon in late afternoon. By trick-or-treat time, it provided ample light for the small children who were canvassing neighborhoods for treats, while at the same time providing an abundance of long, dark, and substantive shadows to hide any goblins or sleeping dogs.

By late evening the little folk had exercised all the doorbells and called it a night. They were home sorting their loot and getting ready for bed. However, the big boys were still roaming about, doing their extemporaneous tricks. They were too old to ask for treats but too young to forget the tricks: tipping toilets, trading buggies between stables, or moving large urns against the outward-opening screen doors at the rear of houses so they couldn't be opened. This would force the occupants to go out the front door and around the house to get to the outhouse in the rear yard, a real handicap when the call was urgent.

This Halloween would be long remembered by Dee Swinehart, a friend of Dad. The moon was now overhead and even the big boys began heading home. Dee was walking up an alley when he spotted the short city marshal making a U-turn and parking in front of the his house. This bothered Dee. "How come Stub can make a U-turn in the street and no one else can?" Dee answered his own question: "Cause he's the marshal"

"Hey, we didn't trick him. How come?" he reasoned with himself. "Cause we're scared of this cocky little man? We all know the motorcycle toughs from Wichita avoid Peabody because of him. The roustabouts from the oil field would rather go to Florence than come to Peabody 'cause of Stub," he remembered.

A few steps farther and Dee had an idea for what he thought would be a great trick for the marshal. Turning, he retraced his steps a block to a corral containing a donkey. The donkey belonged to a large family and was known to be quite gentle. "Now if I can only swipe him without any dogs hearing me," thought Dee.

By now there were few shadows to hide the pair as they headed for Stub's back yard. To keep the donkey's steel shoes from making noise on the alley's gravel, they walked across the grassed rear yards.

Stub had returned home for a cup of coffee since the Halloween activity was about over. "It's been a quiet one this year," he told his wife. He thrust his chin forward and smiled to himself. He was as sure of himself as he was short. Stub's attitude about the evening was about to change, however, as Dee was now leading his new friend through the side yard. Introduction to the donkey would soon happen.

The donkey obediently followed Dee around the house and onto the front porch, a single step. "So far so good," Dee thought as he tied the halter rope to the marshal's front door knob. "Now to ring the doorbell, dash for the alley, and the marshal will meet the donkey face to face. That should be a good trick."

The bell sounded, and Stub wondered, "Who would be trick-or-treating this late? I'll scare the heck out of them." Bending low to look any little kid in the eye, he jerked the door open, stuck his head into the opening, and yelled, "BOOOO..."

The trick worked. The frightened donkey jerked back and the door caught Stub's neck in a very tight squeeze. A standoff resulted. The rope was pulled and remained taut. Neither the marshal nor donkey could or would move.

Dee headed for the next town, Newton, and a movie. As he was going in to find a seat he met Luther, Stub's son, coming out, and they greeted each other. Dee's alibi was in place if he needed one.

The marshal finally got free, and his mood was as sore as his neck. Without a clue about who the trickster was, he offered a fifty-dollar reward, a small fortune in those days, to anyone who helped him solve the crime.

Fifty years later, as an old man, Dee met Stub downtown and asked, "Is the reward for helping find the donkey culprit still a viable offer?"

"'Yer dern right it is. Do you know anything?"

"Hand over the fifty. It was me!"

"Nope, you were in Newton at the theater." Stub had done his detective homework well and still had the case particulars well in mind. Dee couldn't convince him enough to collect.

Tricks can be funny, but there are interesting accidents also. Some accidents are unbelievable!

Chapter 16

"That was Dumb! I Didn't Think"

Experience Doesn't Always Teach

When we were kids, there was a rhyme:
"The Good Lord said, 'I'll pass out brains.'"
Bill, not listening, never fell into line
As he thought the Lord had said trains!

A ndy's not thinking to pull the fuse on the dynamite is an example of "I never tot ob dat!" It nearly cost him his life.

Aunt Ellen said, "If you see Ralph standing in the middle of a field with his hands on his hips and looking at the clouds, you know he's relating to nature by relieving himself." He once was associating with nature in a similar manner near an electric fence. He flipped his outflow toward an insulator, "to wash the dust off it." He later commented, 'I thought all my internal and external organs had been torn apart! I just didn't think.'"

"Dumb things don't happen always in the funny papers," a friend exclaimed. "I saw a fellow in the Korean war take a chainsaw to even up the timbers after we had constructed a bridge. He sat on the end of timber before he cut it. Both he and the saw ended in the river with the remnant of the timber."

Without thinking too long, you can probably remember a time where someone acted without too much thought. If no harm came, it was an incident. When harm occurs, such events are often diagnosed as accidents or misfortunes. How many people have disappeared, or been injured or killed, as a result of not thinking, or, as it is often called, "dumb luck"? Is there a difference between knowing and not thinking, and not knowing and not thinking? Whether the first is negligence and the second is the lack of common sense, the result is often the same as a problem or accident.

It's been said, "Common sense should be on the endangered-species list." To which someone else replied, "The Lord looks after those who help themselves and Uncle Sam helps the rest." In the book, *After the Seventh Day*, by Baron Ritchie-Caulder, the author states the Eskimo may be one of the smarter of the human species. He has to survive with skins and bones as his only tools and his only raw materials. One oversight and it could be curtains. The Eskimo's common sense is well developed. A school principal once suggested offering students a short course in common sense, but no resources could be found: there were no workbooks.

A farmer I knew in my youth, called Sam, had a daughter who married a "city kid." Sam was mowing hay and his son-in-law asked, "Dad, can I help you mow hay?"

"Instead of driving on the cut hay stubble," Sam complained, "the darn kid drove on the standing alfalfa and mashed it to the ground. He just drove all over the field, here and there. Another time he wanted to plow, and he did the same thing. If it took brains to breathe, he would have been dead a long time ago!"

The mountain men, pioneers, and explorers who opened up the wilderness must have had a lot of common sense to survive and to conquer the odds against them. The pioneers who followed and survived also practiced common sense. Knowing that poison could be drawn out of a snake's bite or a lanced boil with wet heat, pioneers sought a warm cow patty, or placed the entrails of a freshly killed fowl on the area.

Andy bought two fattening calves from two maiden sisters. One calf escaped from the barn into the corral. He couldn't get it back into the barn, because it ran from him whenever he entered the corral. He thought a minute and concluded, "I'm not wearing a dress." Going to the house, he asked Nettie, "You got a dress und a bonnet I kin vear?" Dressed as a woman, he had no problem driving the calf into the barn. That is common sense. He could have asked Nettie to drive the calf but he "neber tot ob dat!"

It can be hard to separate fact from fiction, but either one can sometimes make a good story or a point. As Dad sawed hedge wood one day, a neighbor stopped to see him. Seeing the buzz saw, the visitor related a story about a fellow who had an accident with a similar saw and lost a finger. "When the fellow was asked how it happened," the story went, "the guy, without thinking, said, 'Just like that,' and as he swung his hand toward the saw to demonstrate, he lost another finger!" Fact or fiction?

"Dad," I asked as a young boy, "What are those funny-shaped blocks molded of different colored rubber?"

"Grandpa had a Maxwell car and one tire went bad, Dad replied. The casing was OK so he bought a kit of these filler pieces to be put into the tire casing."

"Didn't that ride harder than air in the tire?"

"Yes, but we didn't go very fast either. The first chunks of this so-called 'bologna,' went into the casing easily, but it took a special tool to finish the installation."

Then he told me about the time Grandpa had a problem in Aulne with the Maxwell and its tire filled with bologna. He came home that day with a new tire on the front of the car. Dad asked him why, "Why the new tire?"

"As I vent to turn to leave de town, dhe front veels locked in a durn and I couldn't straighten dem," Grandpa explained. He got nervous but didn't think to slow down. Instead, his foot pushed the gas pedal harder. As a result bystanders, told Dad later, "Andy went round and round in the street until the bologna in the front tire flew out. After finally stopping he went to a station and had a new tire put on the wheel."

"Why didn't you get the bologna tool out of the trunk and put it back into the tire?" Dad asked.

"I neber tot ob dat!"

Whether it was a case of not understanding or not thinking can be argued.

A neighbor boy and his brother were not to marry. Their parents knew the boys' mental capacity was not complete. One of the sons, whose name was Billy, found a girl with nearly the same mental facility, and they sneaked off and were married. Fortunately, his parents had eighty acres where the couple could live. They raised a lot of garden, milked a cow, and had someone else farm the land.

Billy earned a little pocket money by helping Joe Shank, an aged horse doctor. This helper went on calls with Joe to hold animals or tools.

"Momma got a bad case of hemorrhoids one day," Billy's daughter related to a neighbor.

"Did she have any medicine?" the neighbor asked, knowing the family had no horse or car to go to town. Billy and his wife walked to town and carried groceries back the four miles when necessary.

"No, but Daddy used one of the medicines Dr. Shank uses."

"What was that?"

"Turpentine." Billy had often watched the veterinarian pour a little turpentine into melting lard to use on open sores of livestock.

"Did it help?"

"I guess, but it sure got exciting for awhile. Dad had Mom bend over while he poured the turpentine from the can onto her backside. Mom let out a howl. She grabbed a washtub and ran to the well. She pumped water into the tub and sat in it while Dad pumped more water."

As my twin uncles were visiting one Sunday afternoon, one asked the other, "How's Clara Jane's husband Jimmy doing? I haven't seen him for awhile." Jimmy was an independent fellow with a quick and hot temper.

"Well, he pulled a dumb one," the other twin replied. He found a hen he was trying to break of setting. A setting hen is fine if you want the eggs hatched, but Jimmy wanted to sell the eggs rather than hatch them. He threw gasoline on her, and as he turned her loose, he tossed a match at her and yelled, 'Now go and sit, you miserable old hen!' Before she died she ran under his barn, setting it on fire."

"Did he lose his barn?"

"Yup."

Jimmy probably knew better, but he hadn't used common sense. His Irish temper had taken charge.

You would think that having livestock constantly getting out would have caused Herman, our neighbor, to fix his fence, but it didn't. One day, a sow about to farrow wandered down to another farm owned by Pete. Pete shut her in a pen, kept her until she weaned the pigs, and then chased only the sow back to her original home.

That still did not teach Herman a lesson. On a different occasion, a cow got out and wandered to another farm. That farmer saw her coming, and since his electric fence charger was not working, he touched the fence wire to a 220-volt wire. The cow touched the wire and fell dead. Now he probably said, "I knew better than to do that!"

My father-in-law liked to fish after he got off work. He and a buddy would spend an evening at the county lake. One night the friend said as he left to go around behind a bush, "Watch my pole, Emory. I'll be back in a few minutes."

Awhile later the friend complained, "My backside is beginning to smart," and before long, "It's bad now, let's go. Do you reckon I used poison ivy? I should carry toilet paper like you do? I should have known!"

I should have known! How often have we asked ourselves that question? The examples of poor judgment in this chapter cost a person a new tire, two fingers or a terrific jolt when Uncle Ralph tried to wash the electric fence. Imagine the number of fatalities resulting from, "I didn't think, I should have known" or "I forgot!" A proper inscription on their tombstones might be: RIP "I FORGOT."

Grandpa's been gone for decades. I wonder what he would think if he came back to Catlin Township now? Hey, that would make a good assignment for my writing class.

Chapter 17

If Andy Returns

What a Term Paper!

Things have changed, they really have.
If Andy returns he'll need some salve
To remove and ease all the aches and pains
After seeing the changes in the rural plains.

Andrew Larsen arrived in Marion County in 1882 as part of the tremendous surge of population into Kansas. The prairie had been surveyed into sections, with each section having eight eighty-acre parcels. Some of the land was being tilled. However, he bought land that still contained prairie grass that needed plowing, or breaking as it is called when plowed for the first time, and joined his neighbors as a farmer.

A variety of grass species grew on the plains. They were collectively known as prairie grass. Buffalo grass was only three to four inches tall but very tough. A mowing machine had trouble mowing it. The three-to-six-feet-tall big bluestem, the major prairie grass of our area, has been prized for years as pasture for grazing cattle. A shorter bluestem grass is also present. In the early days, trainloads of Texas yearlings would be shipped to the prairie grass of the Flint Hills to become "grass fat" before going onto the Corn Belt to the north for finish fattening.

The Flint Hills is a band of hills and plateaus running across eastern Kansas. U.S. Highway 77 marks the western edge of this region. Ranches and cowboys are still present since the soil and terrain are not suitable for dry land farming.

After settling down to farm, Andy soon saw the dynamic forces of change begin to appear in the new century. He observed how the demographics of the area varied as some farmers became more successful than their neighbors. These farmers prospered and expanded while others could not continue to operate their farms. Tides can vary.

The Standard Atlas of Marion County, Kansas, published in 1921, shows Andrew Larsen owning the four eighty acre parcels on the northern side of section 13 of Catlin Township, while Nettie owned the northern half of the southwest eighty-acre parcel. The neighbor, Joseph Brunk, perhaps had to sell her the north half of his land to afford the large house he built on the south half. This map shows that five farmers were farming section 13 that year. I remember only three farming the section by the early 1930s.

Like the popular game of Monopoly, by Parker Brothers, changes in fortunes began to appear. As the farmers playing the game drew the card, "Go Past the Bank and Buy a Tractor, " things would change even more. As more farmers drew this card, the merchants in towns also noticed tidal changes.

Writing about Andy and the changes in the rural society, I wondered what it would be like to fly to Kansas today and go with my grandfather to Catlin Township and observe the changes together. We have both been gone at least fifty years, Grandpa by death and I by a change of profession.

As I began to think about creating an essay relating such a visit, I wondered how I would plan our meeting for the tour: the depots and bus stations were no longer around. Grandpa would not be familiar with airports, nor had he driven a car other than a Maxwell. "I'll find a way to meet him later as I write the essay," I thought as I went to my word processor. "After renting a car at the Wichita airport I'll drive the forty miles to Peabody."

Now seated, I closed my eyes and began to become creative. "I'll drive down Peabody's Main Street, and stop at the bank corner. Perhaps I'll look up and see him coming out of the bank or coming from the grocery store across the street. I'll figure a way of meeting him as I start to write about such a nostalgic reunion. After seeing him, I'll open the car door so he can get in and the story will begin. As I start to write about our tour, I'll have to plan an itinerary and conversation. As soon as I put some paper in the printer, I'll begin. I'm going to enjoy this essay! I'll have a good paper to read to my writing class next Tuesday."

We made good choices, now for fifty more!

I can't believe it! What's that odd feeling I have? I don't feel sick and yet, I don't feel quite right!

Chapter 18

Andy Returns a Century Later

Unbelievable!

Andy was here to start the prairie's change.
But a visit today would be hard to arrange.
But let's imagine his trip written as an essay,
To observe his surprise and what he has to say.

After a compelling urge to return from California to my Kansas birth area, I flew to Wichita on a red-eye flight and rented a car.

While driving to Peabody with some light music on the radio, I began to sense an odd internal sensation. There was a feeling of elation mixed with a sense of why am I doing this? There were mixed feelings coming from my chest, and some lightheadedness began to be noticeable. "What is happening?" I asked myself as I slowed the car. A phone call the day before assured family and me that son Larry was in good health. Since the natural was OK, could the urge be connected with the supernatural?

The first light of dawn appeared as I drove east just north of Newton. It was late winter and the landscape was barren, abandoned. I saw no signs of livestock or people, other than commuters on the highway and school buses on the rural roads. With only a few schools left in the county buses arrive early in rural areas. The few houses had no smoke rising from their chimneys. The owners must have converted from wood to gas for heat.

Before coming to a stop at the sign on Peabody's Main Street I felt a sense of excitement and euphoria for no reason. Main street had not changed in the past several decades. It was empty of cars except at the street corner on my left. What a century ago had been one of the town's three banks was now being used as The Korner Kitchen. A half-dozen pickup trucks parked near it suggested some farmers were having an early breakfast.

Before entering the intersection, I looked to the right to see if there were any cars coming from that side. There was no car. However, a pedestrian in the crosswalk gripped my attention.

Even before a second look, I was speaking aloud: "I can't believe it!" I mumbled with a shudder. "It's my Grandpa Andy!" As if he recognized me, and perhaps he did, he turned and took several steps towards the passenger door I was opening.

Getting into the car, Grandpa announced, "'ello, Don, I got dis tvlve-'our pass und I vant to visit section t'irteen, Peabody and Aulne, 'en see vat dey ish like better'n a century after I came de first dime. I figured dat you vas de vay to git round to do it."

"I didn't understand my strange feeling that I needed to get to Peabody," was my reply. "Now I think I'm beginning to understand."

"Dat vas arranged."

Morning was just getting started and I was ready for breakfast and a cup of decaf, so I parked at the Korner Kitchen. "Sip of coffee, Grandpa?"

"Koffa? Dis used to be a bank," Grandpa said as we went up the white limestone steps into the cafe. "Der vas tree banks in town in de early days. Chust call me Andy 'stead of Grandpa, as you look olt enough to be a gramp yourself. It vill save a lot of funny looks in 'ere. Let's find a table back in de corner und I'll have vhatever you order for yourself, Don." We sat down and I placed two orders for black coffee and oatmeal.

Remembering how he used to like to put a sugar cube in his mouth and sip coffee through it, I included several cubes in the order. I then removed my coat but he seemed comfortable as he was.

"Vhat in de vorld are all dese farmers doing getting breakfast in 'ere? Vy ain't de eating at home? Vhats wrong vit dem?" Andy hadn't changed during all those years he had been away. "Surely dey have somet'ing to eat at 'ome!"

"I'm surprised at that also," was my reply. "All I can think of is that the wife works in town and they get lonesome. Oh, here comes

Bobby Delk. He is J. J. Delk's son. You remember the Delks that lived two miles west of your place? He's the only one in here that's related to anyone you might remember."

"Let's go to de farm," Andy said as we finished our oatmeal and coffee. "I vant to have a quick look at vere I started," he said as he finished his black coffee. "I vas been back in Odense in Denmark a time or two, but too many tings shanged dere. I vas lost. Dere vas a nice statue of Hans Christian Andersen but de vorkin' vindmills vas all gon."

We drove east two miles on U. S. Highway 50 before I turned north to the southwest corner of section 13. Then I turned east. After a few hundred feet we stopped at the site of the last place Andy and Nettie had lived as a couple - the Brunk Place, as it was known. There was only a tree or two to mark the spot and some broken concrete remaining from the foundation of the house. "Decades ago, before the barn and granary could fall down, Dad took them down in pieces to make sheep shelters on the home place," I informed him.

As we were preparing to leave, Andy turned north and pointed, "Dat's de place vhere your dad's ole buck sheep tried to till me."

"Yeah, I've heard about that."

He sat down on the soil and rubbed his hands over it. "I ain't had dirty fingernails in a 'alf century, Don. Deres no dirt or nail files up dere." With that, he scooped up a handful of soil and threw it up in the air. "De vind still bloos in Kansas. I'm glat I came!" He then got up and started for the car.

Once in the car we drove east a half mile. We stopped and left the car to see if we could find the site where Nettie and her brother, Clyde, had been raised, but to no avail. The buildings and trees had been eliminated a half-century ago.

I turned left at the southeast corner of the section, where Andy batched and later spent the first decade of marriage with Nettie. Turning in the lane I stopped the car. Grandpa opened the door and stepped out. "Dis Kansas air smells goot and de vind is fresh, yust like hit vas a 'undret tventy years ago." After studying the area a few minutes he asked, "Vhat 'appened to de nice ouse Clyde bilt 'ere after buying de farm from me? Udder than a few trees, it looks like dere never had been a farmstead here."

"The buildings were in very poor repair years ago. The last owner didn't need buildings for cash-crop farming so he tore them down."

Andy accepted my answer. Walking to where the center of the farmyard had been, he stopped, crossed his arms, and surveyed his surroundings as if mentally relocating the buildings he remembered. Walking back toward the car he suggested, "Now let's go nort' to de next corner, vhich ve called de Babcock Place, remember?"

"I do. Dad farmed that when I was a boy and a young man."

"Nettie and I lived dere for several years after Louis took ober de 'ome farm."

I had driven north a half-mile when Andy leaned to his left and looked out my window. "Dere's de fence Clyde should 'ave 'elped me build. Did you ebber here ob dat?"

"Yes, Chyde thought that tearing out a half mile of fence to relocate was a poor investment in energy."

Grandpa's head tilted back as he grinned and replied, "Dat vas Clyde alright."

By now we had reached the section line that was once U.S. Highway 50. I turned west a quarter of a mile before I stopped. Opening the gate, I drove into what had once been the farmyard of the Babcock Place.

I could see Andy's look of frustration as he surveyed one more former home site that looked abandoned. "Dere ish nothing left 'ere cept for de vindmill und de tank. Hit's a good ding your dad put 'it all back to pasture. De soil vas never eny goot fer crops. A farmer couldn't live on de crops ee raised 'ere. The prairie should neber have been plowed 'ere."

As we got back into my rental, he looked at me and said. "I vonder if de buffalo wallows are still in de pasture.

"They were fifty years ago when I was still living in Kansas. We had to watch out we didn't drop into one when we drove out there to round up cows."

We were going past the western eighty acres when he commented, "It looks like prairie again."

"Yes, Dad planted it to bromegrass for pasture rather than cropping it."

"Now fer de last place I farmed, de home place."

As we started our three-quarter mile trip west, I warned, "Andy, you'd better be prepared for the changes you'll see. Twenty-five years ago the house you built at the turn of the century caught fire. My son, Larry, and his family were living there then. They got out with only their nightclothes. He filled in the old basement and dug another and used the insurance money to build a smaller house.

Oh, by the way, years ago, Dad and Dave Leppke once worked to straighten some of the stones in the basement walls you laid when you built the house. Dave dropped a hammer behind the wall where they couldn't retrieve it. When cleaning the rubble from the basement before filling it with soil, Larry found Dave's hammer."

"Larry didn't have four kids like ve had, huh? Dat vas a nice house ve built. Ve raised our family dere."

"As did Mom and Dad. But there's more bad news. A tornado came along fifteen years ago. It split into two before it crossed the road south of the driveway. One funnel swung west and took out the Jackson house, while the other funnel leveled everything on the home place: silo, hog house, barn, combine shed, chicken and brooder houses, cattle sheds, granary, and some trees. Tin, boards, fence, trees, and other things were all rolled together. I'm not sure you want to see it. All that was left is your old limestone smokehouse and the new house Larry built. Your fifteen-acre farmstead of out-buildings and corrals is gone. Now the fields come right up to the house and the well."

"Vell, I put a lot ob time, money end sveat into dat place! Let's just go by 'it."

Heading west, I pointed to the left and said, "Dad put the Jackson place all into bromegrass. It had many acres with rock just under the soil. The soil was not very fertile."

"'Dat bromegrass looks a lot like de big prairie grass dat vas here ven I came ober from Denmark!"

We headed north on the Aulne road and Grandpa noticed the approach to the Catlin bridge no longer had the sharp curve of the past. "Dey straightened the road. Hit's bedder."

"The new bridge approach is a lot safer."

After driving around what was left of the small village of Aulne, we parked by the church and leaned against it for a few minutes to talk and remember the past. "Ven you kum out of church you looked at de side of a grocery and cream station building across de street ober dere. Dat building must have bin a hundret feet long. Hit had a community hall upstairs vhere ve always hat a goot time," Andy remembered.

"Deere vas tree or four 'ouses on beyond de community hall as vell as several across de road from it," he continued. "Der all gone, along vith many utters I remember."

"Andy, I did a family history for our children and found an old county atlas that either you or Grandpa Winkley bought. It showed there were probably fifty lots beyond the store. As a boy seventy years ago, I only remember three or four little houses there. Altogether the map had about three hundred lots laid out. I don't know how many were ever sold."

Waving my hand to the south and east, I continued, "Back sixty years ago, when I was a boy, I can remember several businesses here beside the church."

Andy nodded. He mentioned the bank, Kush's butcher shop, Pete Penner's store, a dry goods store, a community phone office, and several others, along with the Rock Island Depot.

"Grandpa, I don't even know the name of the railroad now. It used to be the Chicago, Rock Island, and Pacific Railroad when you lived here. Later it was called just the Rock Island. The same kind of changes hit the Santa Fe rail line. When it started it was the Atchinson, Topeka and Santa Fe. Now I think it is the Burlington Northern Santa Fe. Or perhaps there's been another change in ownership."

Standing on the church's bottom step Andy took one last look around before starting for the car. "Probably Aulne vill neber git healthy again," he said sorrowfully.

"I'd bet with, not against you. Instead of a lot of houses, there's only a few with a lot of lawns between them. The folks living here like to keep their little village neat."

As we walked back to the car, I said, "Grandpa, I think there were a dozen depots in the county in the past, and now there's only one which serves Marion as a library. The same is true of the stockyards, and the section-hands housing that was present in every town. When the railroads disposed of all this property the county had a smaller tax base.

"The railroads lost the need for depots as people bought cars to drive. In your day, people used the local trains to go to the next towns, right?"

He nodded. Continuing, I added, "Cattle are loaded into trucks at the farm and sent directly to market, so stockyards are not needed. Tracks are maintained by machine, so section hands and houses for them are not needed. The process of laying off people in favor of machines is called downsizing in present times. The Santa Fe has taken up one of its two tracks through the county, as trains are longer and there are no passenger trains, unless the continental Amtrak train run by the government leases the route for a daily run."

"With this much tax base gone, the county commissioners have trouble at budget time. Bridge repair isn't affordable, as an example. Many bridges are in poor repair, and some have closed. Some school buses have to detour extra miles twice a day."

Just then we saw a train pass through town. Andy commented, "Hey, 'ee lost de caboose!"

"Nope, more downsizing, Andy. They don't need as many men. The engineer has a radio, and the switches can be thrown for the few passing sidings along the line by a fellow in Wichita."

Andy shook his head at all the changes. "Aulne vas handy in my day. I could send Louis or Bob fer supplies or drive de fat steers de four miles to Aulne a lot quicker den going de six miles to Peabody. It vas a neighborhood town until de cars came along. I 'ate to see Aulne disappear. Dere vas nice people 'ere."

We got into the car and closed the doors. "Drive around Aulne von more time," Andy requested, "and den dake me to Peabody so I can see vut it looks like now. Hits changed too, I spect. I don't neet to see Marion, all ve did dere vas pay de taxes."

As I started the car, I reached in the glove compartment for several candy bars I had purchased at the airport. "I don't know if you can eat the nut bars, Andy, but the big chocolate bar should work if you have teeth problems as you did years ago." The chocolate bar suited him fine.

"Thankee, ve'll git another cuppa coffee ven ve git to town."

He cheered up a bit when we reached Peabody. "Dings don't look neglected," he said as we drove through town to park at the south end of Main Street. "How kum de bridge cross Doyle Creek ish blocked? No money to fix hit, or dit de County commissioners forget Peabody as they used to do?"

"Like I said, Grandpa, a smaller tax base. The improvements on the farms, as on the railroads, are no longer there to help the tax rolls to pay for maintenance."

"Hit's a goot ding dat dey still have taxes frum property in town den."

As we sat in the car I pointed to the first building on the right. "Think about it, Andy, Temple had a car dealership on that corner. It and a lot of new cars were on the tax rolls. There was also a Ford dealer at the other end of the block. There are no car dealers in town now, so no taxes from them. There was a McCormick-Deering farm equipment dealer and a Minneapolis–Moline dealer here with a lot of taxable machinery when I lived here. There aren't any dealers around Peabody now. When I was a boy," I said, "all four larger towns had farm machinery dealers." My memories of the smell of new paint and grease are still vivid.

I got out of the car and as I opened his door, I suggested, "Lets walk across this park made from the Santa Fe depot lot. I wonder if we can find any trace of the depot. Perhaps the paved loading strip remains next to the track."

"You vas right. Dere's only one track left 'ere. Dis used to be a very busy place with passengers un freight coming und going."

Returning toward the car, I pointed to the lot behind the old Temple building, "Do you remember," I asked. "the lumberyard out behind Baker's hardware? The yard had a two-story shed on three sides of the half block. That was full of lumber. Two men with a team of mules and wagon unloaded lumber from a railroad car and stacked it in the yard, board by board. The yard is gone and off the tax roll. Just the big, empty barn remains. Bulgar Boman once had another yard two blocks east."

"Vere do people get lumber now, Don? Newton?"

"Now a truck with the contractor's lumber order from Newton or Wichita comes to your place. With a lift he brought with him, he unloads the truck in a single pass or two and the truck is gone. Losing the stored lumber was more tax money gone and no one is needed to keep the yard stocked by hauling it from freight cars. There's no team of mules to be taxed either."

We returned to the warmth of the car as the late afternoon wind was becoming colder. Grandpa had a puzzled look on his face as he thought about what he was seeing.

"Peabody all but went under a decade or so ago," I said. Only three or four stores were open. Business owners, residents, and a few farmers got involved with a governmental program called Main Street, and things have turned around fairly well. Nobody is making money, but they are holding on and have a good community spirit."

"Vhy can't dey make money?" Andy asked.

As I started the car and began to drive to the park, which was a racetrack years ago, I asked, "Remember how people started going to Peabody and Marion instead of Aulne after the cars arrived on the farm? They passed by Aulne for the larger towns. It's the same process here. Newton and Wichita have more to offer people than Peabody does, and the highway has been improved to make the trips easier and quicker. The highway bypasses Newton so it too is missing some business that goes to Wichita malls."

"Malls?"

"Yeah. They're forty acres of big and little stores and one huge parking lot. They are shopping palaces.

Wrinkling his face and closing his eyes, my companion said with the genuine feeling of a thrifty person, "Palaces made for shopping! Imagine dat! Vot en de vorld ish 'appening to dis country?"

After driving around the old racetrack, I drive to the site of the former stockyards and feed lots Arnold Burns used to receive, fatten, and ship a trainload of cattle at a time. I went past where the native limestone elementary school building used to be, before the site was sold for housing. Going once again to The Korner Kitchen, we ordered more sugar cubes and coffee.

As we enjoyed the repast, I enlarged on the subject of change in the state. "Last fall, Jacquie and I were here for a visit. We left Winfield to return to California. We drove straight west on Highway 160. When we came to a small town, we would turn off the road and drive up the main street. A half or two-thirds of the stores would be closed, with their windows covered with plywood. When we wanted to stop for some bread and meat for sandwiches, we would go to the one remaining store in town. The storekeeper also had fish bait, shirts, rental movies, soda pop, and a few medicines for inventory. By the looks of it, these little stores were not making any money, just existing. One was located on the ground floor of what was once the high school. The owner had put gas pumps in what had been the school front lawn. We then drove through the residential area back to the highway. Many of the houses were not kept in repair and were going downhill. There were a lot of foundations without houses. Peabody certainly looked good after seeing what was happening in these other towns."

"I alvays liked Peabody vhen I vas alive. Vhat's it got going for it now, anyt'ing?"

"Yeah, it has good people. Kurtzie's grandson runs the family bank, and it just expanded and purchased a bank in another town. Hartman Baker's son still runs the mortuary and the furniture store, which are doing fine. People come clear from Wichita to buy furniture. The stores are all operating and the apartments upstairs are being remodeled and rented. Some new houses are being built. Perhaps best of all, the merchants are learning to work together. Peabody may never be a thriving town again, but it looks like it'll be around for awhile longer. The State of Kansas unanimously nominated Peabody for recognition as one of two National Historical towns because of how well the downtown buildings have survived."

"Oh, oh, de sun is startin to go down. Ve bedder git going. My tvelve hour pass ish bout up. How bout vone more cup of coffee and den ve bedder go."

"It's good Sharon had cube sugar for you to put in your mouth to sip your coffee through as you used to do, remember?"

"Yeah, dose vere de days! Hit's gettin late. You 'ave to get back to Vichita?"

"Yes, I will fly from there back to California."

"Vell den, I'll ride along vith you. I kin leave from Vichita yust as vell as from Peabody. I'll enjoy de ride wit you."

As we were driving through Walton, we caught up with a train going our way on the track paralleling the road. As Grandpa turned his head to study the train he wondered aloud, "Vot in de vorld is dat train carrying? Hit looks like a lot ob colored boxes. Dey don't look like cattle cars or boxcars.

"They aren't. Instead of loading individual items into boxcars, manufacturers and shippers load these containers. Tractors with lifts on the front called forklifts transport pallets of goods to the containers, and cranes lift the loaded containers onto trucks or trains for transport."

"Dat's like de combines taking over the binding, shocking, and thrashing of grain."

"Right. It's quicker and a labor-efficient gain for industry."

In thirty minutes we arrived at the airport. After the car was parked in the rental lot, we walked into the lobby so I could turn in the keys. Grandpa gave me a hug, which surprised me, as fifty years ago he was not a demonstrative man. Then he announced, "After tonight you von't remember dis day. Tanks fer de trip!"

I handed in the keys and got my receipt. When I turned around Grandpa was gone!

I walked to my gate without noticing airport displays or people. I was in a time warp of my own and moving in somewhat of a trance. Finding a seat in the lounge, I began to relax.

"Flight 85 is ready to board for Denver and Oakland," an airline person announced. "We'll be leaving in fifteen minutes." I boarded and found my seat. It would be good to lean back and come back to reality.

As we were gaining speed down the tarmac, I looked out my window and saw a tractor working in a field paralleling the runway. Just then he switched on his headlights, as the sunlight had all but faded. It struck me then that I was leaving Andy's time warp. "I'm heading for my own time envelope now, "I realized as I leaned back in my seat.

There was a clunk as the wheels were stowed and the plane banked slightly to the west. We were high enough to catch the last of the sun's rays. Looking downward one more time, I noticed several strings of lights, probably roads. There were also small clusters of light sprinkled here and there, probably farmsteads with chore lights turned on. Later I saw several larger light glows that would be small villages of towns.

I enjoy window seats and I'm glad it was a clear night. I decided to guess my way across the state, seeing if I could remember the roads and towns correctly.

After enjoying the light game for an hour and remembering my visit with Grandpa, I suddenly wondered how John Deere would feel if he could come back for a day as Andy had. This thought led to an even more interesting conjecture: what if Captain John Freemont or Zebulon Pike could be up here with me looking down on the signs of activity in their Great American Desert?

My flight to Oakland was a satisfying one. The anxiety I had suffered twenty-four hours ago was no longer with me. As I lay back in my seat with my eyes closed, I sensed a smile on my face and an inner happiness. I've never had a happier short vacation.

I found myself wondering if I too should plan on returning to the area in fifty or seventy-five years as Grandpa had done. I dozed off with that thought on my mind.

I dozed off but part of my mind continued to function. A Public Broadcasting Service program on change replayed itself on my subconscious viewing screen. First there were the little New England villages building wooden sailing ships. It was a task involving most of the villagers. It was their industry until a neighboring town began to build steel ships. The wooden builders soon ebbed as steel ships became the norm.

The story skipped ahead to the massive effort to have enough ships for World War II. The shipyards were so successful that there was a surplus of vessels at the end of the war, and shipyards went out of business because there were no new orders. The Germans and Japanese built new yards to replace the bombed ones. The new yards were state of the art and American yards weren't able to compete very well. The American shipbuilding industry has ebbed and flowed, as does the tide.

The iron ore and smelting industry of the northeastern states has undergone a similar change. The smelters that once polluted our skies are gone and the iron and steel processing has gone elsewhere.

Just as my body had experienced a long and unusual day, my mind had shared the tension and stress. The video picture in my mind began to dim. But before the sound was gone, I heard the question, "Is this what the automotive industry has been facing for several decades? And a European conglomerate is challenging our aircraft industry in a head-on thrust. What will be nex.....ZZZzzz."

Part Two
Rural Changes

The picture's changed; it's no wonder why.
Changes and efficiency caused some methods to die.
Tractors got stronger, rubber tires gave them speed,
Combines replaced threshing crews to harvest the seed.

Children and hired help were no longer a must.
Work styles changed and machines became a trust.
Downsizing started in rural areas years ago
Before it became a buzzword on the radio.

Children were educated and found urban doors,
Where futures were brighter than a life doing chores.
To continue under the old business plan was to stagnate.
You had to plan, change your ways, or soon capitulate.

Mother changed too, no longer a crew chief or making a bed.
She works in town making payments on the combine instead.
She is now an independent member of the team,
Versed in accounting, database, and self-esteem.

The barn is gone. The hog houses too; there are no hogs.
To see the farmstead, you'd think, it's gone to the dogs.
No cattle, horses, or sheep. It appears it has gone to sleep
The plan's now: plow it, plant it, pray for it, and reap.

No more shocks, corn picking, bangboards, or chickens.
Grandma would say, "It's all gone to the dickens!"
Efficiency did grow and downsizing did spread.
It was necessary to avoid dipping into the red.

What happened to the people who've not left but stayed?
They rolled up sleeves, looked fate in the eyes, and prayed.
Workers, willing, neighborly: an entirely independent crowd.
Forefathers looking down can certainly feel quite proud.

What about the prairies? They're coming back
Not as fenceless bluestem, but as bromegrass, in fact
It's creeping into road ditches where it looks quite nice,
Providing home for pheasant, deer, and little field mice.

Where are the close family ties that across generations grew?
They're all scattered far and wide to start anew.
Grandma's e-mail will be forwarded to a relative's place
And she'll keep up to date with her latest database.

Quick **Order Form**

Fax order: tel 1 800 481-7638

Telephone Orders: Toll free 1 800 481-7638

Have your credit card ready.

Email orders: donlarsen@active-books.com

Postal Orders: Active Books, 358 Lincoln Ave., Livermore, CA, 94550

On-line orders: www.active-books.com

❑ **Please send the following books:**

_____ *Prairie Tides* at $14.95 $_____._____

_____ *I've Never Been an Old Man* at $19.95 $_____._____

_____ Set of Both Books at $25.95 $_____._____

I may return any books for full refund, no questions

Sales tax: Please add 8.75% for books shipped to CA   ($_____._____)

Shipping: Flat $2.00 Active Books will cover the balance $2.00

Total $_____._____

Send to:

Name _____

Address _____

City_____ State_____ Zip _____

Telephone _____

Email _____

Payment:

❑ Check; ❑ Credit card; ❑ Visa; ❑ MasterCard; ❑ Discovery

Card number: _____ Expires: ___/___/___

Name on card: _____

Signature of crad Holder:_____

ACTIVE BOOKS

Non-Fiction People Aging
Illness Caregiving Dementia

I'VE NEVER BEEN AN OLD MAN

What it's Like if You Plan to Age

Don Larsen

Foreword by
Dr. Grace Devnich

How much do you know about aging? With humor and insight Don Larsen teaches:

- **the benefits of love and close friendships in later years,**

- **the important role of pets in bringing comfort to both ill and healthy persons, and**

- **the value of active participation—not just toleration—in the process of aging.**

"*I've Never Been an Old Man: What It's Like if You Plan to Age* is an engaging first-person narrative of the trails and travails of growing old. While not a self-help book per se, readers will almost certainly glean insight in coping with the difficulties that come with loss of faculties, and the long-term value of actively embracing aging rather than simply tolerating it. Chapters speak of doctor's office fiascos, lifelong milestones, "cat husbandry with no degree" and more. A chuckle-inducing and emotionally uplifting as well as practical-eyed tour de force of the golden years of life."
—*James A. Cox, Editor-in-Chief*
Midwest Book Review

- "*What a pleasure to read your book! It gave me insight in dealing with my 86-year-old dad, as well as preparing me for my 'future years.'*"
—*Marilou Mazotti, caregiver and teacher*

- "*Don brings humor into an emergency room, love into an older marriage, strength from his coffee cats, and encouragement to those who are aging.*"
—*Dorothy Womack, author of* Alzheimer's Angels

- "I've Never Been an Old Man *is much more than a first-person narrative about the challenges of aging. It is an inspiring love story energized by author Don Larsen's passion for life. His upbeat writing style, gentle humor, and cliff-hanger chapter endings will keep readers turning pages.*"
—*B.J. FitzRay, author of* Alzheimer's Activities

Don teaches us about life, love, and the ABC's of IVs and HMOs, while his cats...uh, family members, add hilarity.

Buy a book for yourself plus a copy for the Baby Boomer who may someday care for you!